LEGACY

A Family Guide to Generational Wealth

Legal & Disclaimer

The content and information in this book are consistent and truthful. They have been supplied for informational, educational, and business purposes only.

The content and information contained in this book have been compiled from reliable sources, which are correct based on the author's knowledge, belief, and expertise.

The author cannot be held liable for any omissions and/or errors. I am not a financial advisor, and nothing in this book should be taken as financial advice. Do your own due diligence. I am not responsible for any investments or losses from the following suggestions in this book.

Acknowledgments and Dedication

The God in my life saved me to help my family and community.

This book is a gift to my children, my bonus children, grandchildren, nieces, nephews, and all who call me their "parent" and who have made me a part of their village.

I hope the wisdom you gain from this book allows you to avoid the pitfalls of life. Stay on the narrow path of life, but if you must choose between doing right or wrong, always choose right.

To my love and my other half -

Thank you for being patient and supportive of me and all my endeavors. You are a miracle, and your presence blesses me.

Special acknowledgment to my entrepreneur grandfather, Joseph Barnes. He paved the way for us where no one looked like him.

Joseph Barnes, a wealthy entrepreneur in the 1950s, owned a restaurant and real estate. Following his death, his estate helped my grandmother and his many family members. This Family Guide to

Generational Wealth recognizes all his hard work and the legacy he left to his children and grandchildren.

In memory of my mother Elaine Smith, my guardian angel.

To my brothers, uncles, aunts, cousins, and the people who helped raise me: I appreciate you for helping me throughout my life and leading with class, integrity, and morals.

To my village, this book lets you know you mean the world to me. I could not have raised my son without your help. To all my friends, you know who you are, there would be no "me" without "you."

Now all glory to God, who is able, through his mighty power at work within us, to accomplish infinitely more than we might ask or think."

- Ephesians 3: 20

My motto is: Be the person you needed when you were growing up.

To all parents: Sometimes your greatest contribution to the world is not what you do, but whom you raise and all those you gave nuggets of wisdom.

To all children: I designed this book to put you on the right path so that handling finances becomes second nature from an early age and for generations to come.

Legacy

Legacy stamps your future, contributing to future generations. People want to leave a legacy to feel that their life mattered.

A legacy has a lasting impact on the world. It can be money, property, or even stories and memories. It's a gift passed down through generations.

It can also be a business – or the profits from a business, set up in a foundation or charity. *Leaving a legacy* means dreaming big and changing the world for the better.

Generational Wealth

Generational Wealth includes financial assets or other things passed down to younger generations. It refers to stocks, real estate, cash, education, and even entire businesses. Wealth passed down may occur after the death of family members or while they still live.

"Intelligence can create huge profits, and in fact, you can make more money being smart than you can being strong or fast."
Robert Smith

Table of Contents

INTRODUCTION... 1

INTRODUCTION TO TEACH CHILDREN 11

STEP ONE: SAVING MONEY 19

STEP TWO: MONEY MINDSET..27

STEP THREE: MAKE MONEY WORK FOR YOU.......................43

STEP FOUR: INVEST LIKE THE WEALTHY 61

STEP FIVE: THE POWER OF BUDGETS, INSURANCE & TAXES....... 79

STEP SIX: ALL ABOUT CREDIT...89

STEP SEVEN: BE A PRODUCER 107

STEP EIGHT: THE ART OF NEGOTIATING............................117

STEP NINE: DO WHAT YOU LOVE & HELP WHOM YOU CAN.........125

STEP TEN: EDUCATION 135

BLUEPRINT TO START AND MAINTAIN A REAL BUSINESS!............ 163

ABOUT THE AUTHOR..188

WORKS CITED 189

Introduction

This family guide to generational wealth owes a great debt to my heritage. Like other analysts and authors on this subject, multiple factors have shaped my person and perception − my ancestors; the history, legends, and experiences unique to my family; the circumstances of the social evolution affecting the United States, the City of Philadelphia, and my neighborhood; and much more. I can only try to think and act at some distance from these circumstances.

For example, I come from a family typical of many families in a low- to middle-economic class. I have benefitted from hearing stories of my grandfather's legacy acquired throughout the Civil Rights era. My grandfather Joseph Barnes moved from Mississippi to Philadelphia, where he owned two restaurants in the 1940s. My grandmother Dorothy was a wise woman, an extraordinary cook, and a hostess at the restaurant. Ultimately, Dorothy urged Joseph to meet with the other businessmen in the community and attend business meetings. My grandmother also helped manage the money from the restaurant. Before my grandfather got sick and passed away, he acquired 17 properties, stocks, bonds, and several other assets (see photos in the back of the book for a list of properties, assets, and will pages: 185-187). I was told that my grandfather split the assets between many of his family members and left my grandmother houses and other things, with one home remaining in the family to this day. His children (Elaine, Joseph, and Sandra) continued the legacy of investing, saving, and hard work, allowing them to live comfortable lives and pass their wealth and wisdom to others. Joseph Barnes children helped family members through college and were able to accomplish various other things. My children and I have adopted these principles and are passing this knowledge to peers through businesses and non-profits. The local newspaper wrote an article about my grandfather because of his many achievements in the 1960s. Many legacies do not last beyond one generation, which inspired me to write this book!

I was the second to get a college degree in my family, which widened my vision of different world views.

I understand that my perspective is only one of many and may differ from others. But writing this book has widened the world I hope to reach. If, for instance, it does not specifically address the needs of those struggling to keep their families together, I still believe the lessons promoted here can nourish their wants and needs.

Having said this, I believe parents work to ensure their children learn to read, write, and make sound life decisions. However, it's also my experience that parents and schools often do not teach their children about money. This one thing will make the difference between financial success and failure in the typical modern family. We want them to become responsible adults.

Now, having money is only part of it. Money's value does not compare to love, faith, health, friendship, peace, and security. It does not replace the joy of a baby's first cry or a first love's passion. Please do not mistake my position. I do not believe money can buy happiness.

But I hold that "the lack of money can buy a heap of misery!" Edmund Burke, the Irish Member of England's parliament at the time of America's rebellion, said something similar:

> *"If we command our wealth, we shall be rich and free. If our wealth commands us, we are poor indeed."*

Families regard money as personal and private, so they avoid discussing it. As a result, children leave home without the necessary skills for financial security and success. This failure of communication − and the fears attached − reinforce cycles of financial illiteracy in the following generations.

When I talk to people about money, they invariably say, "If I knew then what I know now, I would be rich." They might agree with Sophie Tucker, a vaudeville entertainer in the middle of the last century, who said,

"I've been rich, and I've been poor. Rich is better."

I can relate to that sentiment. We may make poor financial choices early in life, which cost us later. And some of us continue to pay for those mistakes today!

Others do not make any significant blunders. Still, they must take the necessary steps toward financial literacy and economic freedom. As a result, they may seem comfortable. But they are far from where they could have been if they had known and applied the best practices in financial health and wealth.

Then, there is a third group. They continue to dig the hole they started years ago! They have yet to learn how to manage their money and still need to know the basics. I like the quote attributed to Albert Einstein, the most influential physicist of the 20th century,

"The definition of insanity is doing the same thing over and over and expecting different results."

We can and must leave a different legacy for our children, a legacy including financial literacy. For example, we must stop selling the homes our parents or grandparents passed down to us.

Instead, we should pass them from generation to generation to create, keep, and pay forward generational wealth. This legacy calls for a transformational change in our economic thinking and behavior. It requires a new mindset.

We must transform our thinking about how we manage our money. The necessary transformation does not create something new. Instead, it takes what you have and makes it different and better.

Take butterflies, for example.

After living one life, doing little but crawling, eating, and preparing for their big show, caterpillars build cocoons to change their shape and purpose. They offer inspiration and model what it truly means to transform. Inside cocoons, the caterpillar's body falls apart, reserving parts of itself and reshaping them into a butterfly. The butterfly takes what it already has inside its paper-thin shell and uses it to grow until the space inside is too small to hold it. Cramped and squeezed, it pokes and pushes with its wings and limbs, building strength with these actions.

Therein lies the second lesson the butterfly teaches: *If we help the butterfly in the struggle to get out of its cocoon, we sign its death warrant.* Ask kindergarten teacher Marcie Hinton. She left her pre-K children alone with a butterfly enclosure she had bought to teach the children about the caterpillar-to-butterfly life cycle.

It took Ms. Hanson just a moment to briefly talk with another teacher who had stopped by her classroom. During that time, the children had lovingly poked holes in the nine cocoons hanging from the top of the enclosure. The students had seen little body parts pushing their way through the shell and wanted to help them.

But the butterflies needed that struggle to grow wings strong enough to fly. When Ms. Henson returned, nine of the ten butterflies lay struggling on the enclosure floor. Only the tenth one had to fight its way out, developing the strength to flap its wings later and fly away.

Becoming financially stable and monetarily free requires work on our part. We must go through this transformation process with our children. If we do not, we will fail to model the good behaviors that result in money health. Most children will do as we do, *not as we say*. Whatever we do in front of our children becomes a habit for them. We must set an excellent example about money and finances for our children because they are always watching us. That is where good habits start!

I'm inspired by the words of Indian author and activist Shiv Kera:

"Your positive action combined with positive thinking results in success."

Back to the butterfly! A caterpillar eventually punctures the cocoon's walls, once its own body. It hangs out on the tree branch for a while, dries its wings, and practices flapping; then, it lets go, trusting those wings will carry it away.

When we consider avoiding change, either because of the pain or the fear of the unknown, we should remember this example of what it takes for true transformation and move on with the task. Like the butterfly, after some discomfort, we will soar!

It does not take a degree in economics to teach the fundamentals of money management. The same principles your children learn here will work for you. Simple but essential rules go a long way toward instilling fiscal responsibility in your child. This knowledge will help them become self-assured and financially self-sufficient individuals.

If you set a strong, solid financial example for your children, they should grow up financially responsible. That strengthens the family today and for generations to come. As the lovely scripture Proverbs 2: 6 reminds us,

---

"Train up a child in the way he should go, and when he is old, he will not depart from it."

Set aside time to read these concepts with your child, take part in the activities, and help your child follow the exercises.

We all learn to count money in elementary school. However, we must understand how money works, how it grows, and how to use it responsibly. You must teach your children the dollar value and, eventually, about currencies from other countries.

How do you do this? You can teach your children financial literacy. I will outline the basic concepts everyone should know in the coming pages. But once you know them, you must teach your children to do the same.

Apply these concepts to your finances. Children learn best by example when mixed with sound principles.

- Teach your children that they are *heirs*. As heirs, they should respect whatever fortune – big or small – you can leave.

- Teach your heirs to live below their means. They must not spend more than they earn. They should not live to impress. For example, this means not upgrading your car to compete with neighbors.

- Understand that an inheritance given too early in life does not prove a blessing. Wealth generally does not last past the second generation.

A groundbreaking study by The Williams Group[1] explored the behavior of 3,200 families. Their researchers found seven out of 10 families lose their inherited fortune by the second generation. Nine in

---

[1] (Moran, 2021)

10 lose it by the third generation. However, careful planning can beat these negative odds:

- Set up your estate to keep heirs from blowing their inheritance before age 21. Neurologists agree that a person's brain does not develop fully until age 25, so don't expect them to be able to make completely sound money decisions. That's why rental companies don't rent to people under 25.

- Stipulate in your will that heirs cannot touch their inherited wealth until a certain age when the inherited wealth will have accumulated interest or dividends.

- Set the will up to issue specific amounts of inheritance at ages 30, 40, and 50. This allocation of the estate sustains and optimizes your legacy.

Prepare a strategic plan for wealth growth and distribution with the advice of a lawyer and **Certified Financial Adviser**. It would help if you had advice on setting up a trust fund, a decision that will save you money in the future.

Self-worth does not lie in money or possessions. *Money is a tool that helps people create the life they want, not the life others want them to have.* Being humble, frugal, and sensible will sustain and grow your legacy of generational wealth.

The key to financial freedom is to start now. Every second you delay costs you a fortune!

Instructions

I have designed the following content so you can **cover it with your Family**. Each chapter opens with instructions and ends with ways to support your child in learning the concept. However, children can read both sections also if they are ready.

We want to hear about your journey. Let us know where you start and finish so we can celebrate your success.

What the rich teach their children.

"I have five dollars that says you won't give me a shot and we'll sweep this little matter under the rug."

"Money does not buy you happiness, but lack of money certainly buys you misery."

— Daniel Kahneman, Well-Being: Foundations of Hedonic Psychology

Hey everyone!

Congratulations on taking the path toward wealth! You will learn things essential for your life - now and in the future. You will find this manageable. You need to understand what to do. You can do this! Step-by-step, you will learn how to build a fortune!

Money isn't all there is to life. Family, friends, faith, education, and fun are essential. But you need money to do what you *must* do and what you *want* to do.

You can start by answering these questions:

- What do you want to do with your future?

- What are your goals?

- What career do you want to pursue?

- What kind of house do you want to live in?

- What type of car would you like to drive?

- Where would you like to vacation, and what friends or family would you like to take with you?

You should answer these crucial questions now. The answers will set goals to help you stay motivated.

Say, "Thank you!"

Before we start, take a minute to say "thank you" to the adult who bought this book for you or yourself if you bought it to educate yourself. That person knows your life will be more fun if you have a robust financial education. School teaches you science, history, vocabulary, and math. But few classes talk about how money works. That is why some very educated people do not keep their money!

> ### *Formal education will make you a living: self-education will make you a fortune. Jim Rohn*

You, however, will have financial knowledge along with book knowledge. And you will know how to make money, save, invest, and use your money to carry out your goals long before you even get your first job!

It would be best if you worked with an adult as you practiced the steps in this guidebook. If your parent or guardian is not available, it's okay. Ask a teacher, aunt, uncle, grandparent, or trusted family friend if you need help understanding something. Never be afraid to ask questions. The only dumb questions are the ones not asked. Also, you can now use Google or Bing to search for things on the internet – with your parent's permission.

You will discover what fun managing your money can be and learn the skills to make wise financial decisions. You can play money games and try to understand a new concept or term daily. Make it rewarding. No need to worry; you can do this. We will get through it together.

Children as young as three or four years can understand basic money concepts. If you're old enough to count, you can discuss learning, spending, investing, and saving your money! And think of all the things you can do, places you can go, and people you can help if you have the money.

You can buy everything you want with an intelligent spending system, including video games, controllers, virtual currency, and more. There will be space in the budget for everything your parents think is necessary and the things you find fun!

Some children do so well with their money that they become millionaires in their teens. But no pressure! You don't have to be a millionaire to be a smart money manager. **Every dollar you can add to your bank account makes you financially stronger – and more independent!**

The most important lesson I want you to learn is that wealth is your right! Although some communities struggle today, it was not always that way. You may not know this, but there was a time when persons of color were among the wealthiest people in the world.

Systems like racism, economic repression, and war have too often turned the financial lives of minorities upside down. For example,

- Slavery throughout regions of the United States deprived African Americans of property. But by the 1920s, Black people had bought real estate, started businesses, and run banking and investment companies. For example, successful Black retail and financial institutions lined Tulsa, Oklahoma's Black Wall Street.

  However, on May 31, 1921, The Black Wall Street Massacre began. Hundreds of Black residents died at the hands of White vigilantes. Thirty-five square blocks of prosperous homes and businesses burned to the ground. The Burning of Black Wall Street set many families back financially, destroying their wealth, and plunging them into poverty for generations.

- U.S. treaties with Native Americans pushed them onto reservations where most live today. From the late 1800s to the early 1900s, "the federal government parceled millions of acres of Native American lands to individual Native Americans."[2]

  The passage of the General Allotment Act of 1887 effectively minimized the potential for individual Native American wealth. While the federal government allotted 80 to 160 acres to individuals, the government held those allotments in trust.

---

[2] (Native American Ownership and Governance of Natural Resources, 2022)

When the allocated acres fell out of the trust, the land became taxable, causing "thousands of acres of Native American land to pass out of Native American hands."[3]

As a result, the allotted acreage has often fallen into the hands of a tribe, multiple tribes, Native Americans, and non-Native Americans. "In many cases, ownership of allotted lands continued to divide over multiple generations so that today, individual parcels sometimes have more than 100 co-owners."[4]

- After the Japanese military attack on Pearl Harbor in 1941, systemic racism and fears of Japanese espionage prompted President Franklin Roosevelt to order the "internment," also known as the imprisonment of 110,000 plus Japanese American citizens in ten "camps."

Incarcerated within three days of the 1944 order, these citizens lost their homes, cars, and businesses. This effectively ruined the existing personal and business wealth of the internees. But the internment of up to three years also reduced earning and career potential.

"Twenty-five years after the internment camps, Japanese-American men's earnings were between 9% and 13% lower

---

[3] (Native American Ownership and Governance of Natural Resources, 2022)
[4] (Native American Ownership and Governance of Natural Resources, 2022)

than they should have been."[5] People of Japanese descent lost $149 million and $370 million (in 1945 dollars) in income and property valued at over $7.88 billion in 2022.[6]

Despite such examples of economic deprivation, your generation will find it easier to achieve and secure wealth for an enterprising adult of any color or ethnicity. There was a time when most minorities became wealthy in sports, politics, and entertainment. Today, you can freely explore inventions, education, investment, and entrepreneurship. Owning a business has never been more accessible. Barriers that held back dynamic, industrious people have eased. Systematic barriers for people of color still exist. People still act with bias in other ways, such as sexual orientation. Today's social context requires you to work harder or smarter than the next person to stand out. My grandmother used to say, "The cream always rises to the top."

So, as we prepare to take this fantastic journey together, remember this ancient proverb, often attributed to the 19th-century English novelist Ann Isabella Thackeray Ritchie:

"Give a person a fish, and he will eat it for a day. Teach a person to fish, andhe eats for his entire lifetime."

---

[5] (Guilford, 2022)
[6] (Guilford, 2022)

You are about to learn skills you can use to create wealth that lasts a lifetime! We will talk at length about money because it is important. But self-worth does not lie in money or possessions alone.

It would help if you were first loving, humble, frugal, and sensible. Money is still a tool, one that helps people live the life they want. Health and kindness remain more important than money.

Money only makes you more of what you were before you earned it. If you are selfish, money only makes you more selfish. But if you are a good person, money can help you do better in the world.

I encourage you to use what you learn to build a legacy of wealth that you can pass down to your children and their children, teaching them to value money as well as all the things money cannot buy.

Step One
Saving Money

"Money isn't everything...but it ranks right up there with oxygen."

—Humorist and Author Rita Davenport

You might be thinking, "I don't have any money; how can I save it?"

Well, you do have access to money from time to time. Babysitting jobs, allowances, chore money, birthday money, and other monies you receive represent your *income*. **Income** refers to the money that comes to you from any source. As you enter your teenage years, you might also get a job where you will have a steady income. Later, we will cover ways to make money, no matter how old you are.

Income = money received, especially regularly, for work or through investments.

However good your income only matters if you have a habit of *saving*. It is the most important of all the practices you will learn. So, let us discuss how to save.

No matter how old you are - from nine to 99 - you should start by setting aside a percentage of the money you earn. Young children often enjoy putting coins and dollars in a jar or piggy bank. This allows them to see their money grow. Still, other kids prefer to save money in an account with a bank (or savings and loan).

No matter your age, the bank will let you open an account with your name, even though you may need a parent to sign the paperwork. It might help to set a specific goal to save up to buy something you want. But it's best continually add to the core savings you never touch.

A bank account gives people a safe place to save money for the future, and most savings accounts pay little interest.

Interest = a small payment the bank deposits into your account based on your account balance.

If you deposit a little in the bank, the bank will pay you for letting them hold onto your money. Why would they do that? Well, your money does not just sit in the bank. They only keep a little bit of money in the physical bank for day-to-day transactions.

The bank takes your money and invests it. The money deposited goes into ventures where the bank thinks they can make money. Banks pay you *interest* for letting them use your money in this way.

There are three kinds of banks: brick-and-mortar, virtual, and hybrid. Hybrid banks are a combination of the other two.

1. ***Brick-and-mortar*** banks have one or more physical locations. You can go to the bank to deposit or withdraw money.

2. ***Virtual banks*** function 100% online. They do not have physical "branches" or brick-and-mortar buildings. Customers do everything by phone, on a computer, or through an app.

3. Most banks today have ***hybrid infrastructures***. You conduct most transactions online but can go into the bank building if you need or want to.

Bank accounts are a wonderful place to save and grow money. For example, suppose you get a $20 per week allowance for doing your chores and want to buy a new bike. You might put ten dollars toward your ongoing savings and ten dollars toward the bicycle.

Never let your savings account balance go to zero to buy something you want!

Teaching yourself to save will follow you into adulthood and ensure you always have money to meet your needs. You never know when an emergency or an opportunity might arise. If you have money saved, you can address the crisis or take advantage of the opportunity. If you do not, you must scramble to figure something out. You should have an emergency fund. While the size of your emergency savings will vary depending on your lifestyle, most experts believe you should put away at least three to six months' worth of living expenses.

You may find saving money a challenge. It's hard to have money and resist the urge to spend it. However, you must develop this skill. Most people don't have good money habits because they did not learn them as children. So, if you did not learn about saving before, be thankful that you know it now.

Exhibit 1: The Thirds Rule

An excellent rule for savings is to break your money into pieces. One method is by using The Thirds Rule illustrated here in Figure 1:

Save for a Goal

Spend Now

Save & Invest

Adults can use this formula, too! Let's use $30 to make the math easy. You might put ten dollars in your pocket for whatever you want. Another ten dollars could go into your savings account for future purchases. But you should save the remaining ten dollars as an investment. We will talk more about that later.

Instead of breaking your income into thirds, you might also set aside a chunk of money to give away. Following The Fourths Rule, you might give the fourth piece to a church or community organization important to you. You might use the money to sponsor a child in an impoverished country or donate to an organization doing important work worldwide. See Exhibit 2:

Exhibit 2: The Fourths Rule

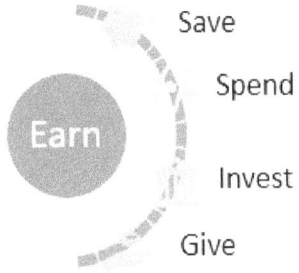

Save

Spend

Invest

Give

If you find it hard to save, start small. Can you save a couple of dollars a day? $5 per day equals $150 a month? If you don't have access to that much money, you can decide to save a portion of every source of income. If you start saving even a small amount early in life, it will add up over time. Social scientists studied the $5 per day or $150 per savings strategy.[7] They found a huge psychological advantage for the little-bit-every-day habit. They also found that low-

---

[7] (Herschfield, Shu, & Benartzi, 2019)

income savers could save at the same rate as high-income users when they followed the $5-a-day plan.

It doesn't matter which way you save. Just pick one and start saving soon! Committing to saving at least 10 percent of your income would be best. You have to have a plan for life. If you fail to plan, then you plan to fail!

The 10% Way

You can be much happier if you make this 10 percent savings a rule − and never break it. You will stay leaps and bounds ahead of most people you know.

Imagine your future! Visualize your future self, enjoying your savings! Picture yourself living in a big house, succeeding in business, or taking a dream vacation. See yourself in those situations! Build a Dream Board.[8] Glue cuttings from magazines and your drawings to a large poster board and hang it on a wall where you can see it daily. Before you know it, you'll look around and see what you put on the Dream Board has come to life. Later, you will learn to save and invest more than you spend to always have money available.

---

[8] (Conlon, 2022)

Saving

If you do not listen to any other advice, take the advice to become a saver very seriously.

1. **Shop "big box" discount stores** where surplus building materials, appliances, used furnishings and bulk items are sold at low prices. Costco or Sam's Club may be cost-effective if you have a big family. They often offer other free services.

2. **Explore second-hand shops**. Thrift and second-hand stores have great finds, especially for children who outgrow things fast. You can buy name brands for up to 90% off retail prices.

3. **Watch out for quick money scams**: If someone offers you something for nothing, it's likely a **scam**. Suppose someone promises to deposit money into your bank account if you buy a gift card. It's a **scam**. If an email pleads for your money, it is a scam. Scammers target people through gift cards, wire transfers, bitcoin addresses, cash, and peer-to-peer apps. These money exchange apps are for people who know each other, so do not send money to strangers. Period!

So, that's the end of the book. Just kidding!

There is more to discover because you must know what to do with the money you save and how to make even more money.

Summary

In this section, children learn about saving money at home, in a little safe, or in a back account you help them open. Model and instill good money habits. Your efforts will benefit children for the rest of their lives. The best way to teach is to lead:

+ Start a savings plan if you do not have one.
+ Put savings on autopilot, depositing a set amount from every paycheck.
+ Refinance student loans.
+ Use coupons and search for discounts.
+ Buy second-hand instead of new whenever you can.
+ Avoid quick-money scams with their high interest and fees.

Step Two - Think Differently
About Wealth

"Financial peace isn't the acquisition of stuff. It is learning to live on less than you make so you can give money back and have money to invest. You can't win until you do this."

- Radio Show Host, Author, and Businessman Dave Ramsey.

Remember to give. Like Robert F. Smith who is a billionaire. He started from humble beginnings and now owns a hedge fund. But Smith's persona is much more than just his hedge fund. He is known for his philanthropic work – like his donations to HBCUs, paying off the student loans for Morehouse graduates, and his work in combatting prostate cancer in the community. We want to be conscious of giving back to those less fortunate. Money gives us a way to help others. Don't give away the last dollar in your pocket. Always make sure you are stable first.

Wealth Building

Now that you have the habit of saving under your belt let's talk about a big concept regarding building your financial legacy: **Wealth Building.**

Wealth = Abundance

The dictionary defines "wealth" as "the abundance of money or possessions." But you can have an abundance of anything of value:

- Abundance of friends
- Abundance of family
- Abundance of knowledge

- Abundance of spirituality
- Abundance of generosity
- Abundance of peace
- Abundance of freedom

When you have these things and add money or possessions to the mix, you have the foundation of an extraordinary life. The money and possessions you own make up your ***financial wealth***. But we are not just interested in having wealth for today. ***Creating a Legacy means building wealth that lasts even beyond your lifetime***. We call this ***Generational Wealth***.

Generational Wealth transfers financial wealth from one family member to the next. The wealth earned by one generation passes down to the next. For example, your grandparents may leave you an inheritance, house, or business. Generational Wealth may include valuable assets, such as cash, real estate, rare coins, jewels, securities, rare books, investments, or family businesses.

However, history proves how difficult it is to sustain Generational Wealth across generations. The Deloitte Center for Financial Services predicts, "Over the next 15 years, nearly $24 trillion will be transferred in bequests (after taxes and charitable giving), reflecting spousal, inter- and intra-generational wealth transfers."[9] However, the report estimates "70% of wealthy families will lose their wealth

---

[9] (Srinivas & Goradia, 2015)

by the second generation, and 90% will lose it by the third."[10]
Lessons taught in this book can help you beat these odds!

The Wealth Mindset

Wealth is so much more than material things. It also refers to your **Mindset** about money. You must pass down a positive attitude about money from one person to another. Your money mindset might range from pursuing *excessive prosperity* to holding that *the "love" of money is the root of all evil*. The truth lies somewhere in the middle. But a person's mindset about money directly affects their current and future financial situation. People can do good things with money or destroy their lives and the lives of others with it.

Money opens doors to opportunities. Being financially secure reduces stress, leaving you free to focus on other things. It also becomes a tool to improve things in the world rather than just a way to buy luxury items like Gucci or Rolex.

Rappers, movie stars, basketball players, and big corporate CEOs live lavish lifestyles flaunting their bling, yachts, parties, and designer clothes. It looks like they "have it made" because they have everything money can buy.

---

[10] (Kleinhandler, 2018)

You may want to emulate famous and rich people, but you should never envy them. These people are just like you and me. They have problems, health concerns, parenting issues, marriage problems, and mental health struggles, too.

Wealth comes with a price. Keep that in mind as you read and think about the money you want someday.

How much money is considered generational wealth?

Good question! The short answer is *any amount* you choose to sustain your family, but according to Charles Schwab, the average net worth of an American to be considered wealthy is 2.2 million.[11] You should not measure wealth by a family's millions. Instead, *you measure wealth with a positive mindset about money.*

Thomas J. Stanley, an author of *The Millionaire Next Door*, created the "wealth equation."[12] It multiplies 10% of the age of the highest income earner in the household times the household's joint income to calculate your expected net worth (ENW).

---

[11] (Bradbury, 2022)
[12] (Stanley & Danko, 1996)

$$ENW = \frac{\text{Your Age X Pre-tax Annual Household Income}}{10^{13}}$$

People often blame their lack of money on the circumstances surrounding them. However, sometimes we create these circumstances. And a negative money mindset plays a significant role.

People struggle with negative money mindsets every day. They say, "Money doesn't buy happiness," "Money doesn't fall from the sky," and "Money doesn't grow on trees." Adults in my life often said such things instead of simply explaining where and how to accumulate money and how saving solves some problems.

Erase those negative statements from your mind!

Money is easy to come by legally, morally, and ethically. Yes, it requires work. But it is only one of the challenges you will face.

When you were younger, an adult might have read *The Little Engine That Could*. A century old, this treasured book tells the story of a little train climbing a hill to deliver toys and food to the village below. The book centers on one phrase:

---

[13]Dr. Stanley admits this equation has limitations and is just an interesting rule of thumb for people over 40.

I think I can.

I think I can.

I think I can.

I think I can.

The little train repeated this phrase until it climbed the hill and made it to the top! These words become an affirmation for the train.

Please choose one of these powerful affirmations and repeat it daily for incredible results.

1. I am strong!
2. I am smart!
3. I can change the world!
4. I am a magnet for money!
5. More money is due to me!
8. I am open and receptive to all life offers!
9. I want money to better myself and the lives of others!
10. Money is my servant!

Repeating such statements will not make you rich, but it will affirm you know these things are possible. Hearing yourself say positive things is more important than anything others say. Cheer yourself on when no one else does. Look in the mirror and motivate yourself. Say along with Olympic medalist, Golden Gloves Champion, and US Featherweight Champion Floyd Mayweather, Jr:

"Money doesn't make me; I make money!"

Children who inherit generational wealth have an advantage over those who do not. But again, you can catch up by learning about money. Their inheritance can go towards other income-generating assets that appreciate. You can use it for college or buy your first home. Without inherited wealth, you will have to start at zero and build wealth, but that is all right, too. You now have the tools.

The key to financial freedom is to start now. Every second you wait, you are delaying your fortune!

Even if you have not received help from money passed down, don't worry. You can start today on your road to wealth so you will have something to pass down to your children. ***The legacy can start with you!***

In the next chapter, we are going to talk about how to make money. But there is one more important mindset lesson you must learn:

Character is far more important than money.

A rich person may have friends, but not all those friends will be there for them if they lose their riches. Loyal friends are there for you whether you are rich or poor.

Do not share all your successes with everyone. It's not a good idea to advertise that you have money on social media sites. Some people will not be happy for you. It is just a fact.

- People will fake liking you to get near you for the things you have.

- People who are not on the same level as you will think that you're bragging.

- And others will let the jealousy, the green-eyed monster consume them.

It's important to know who your real friends are when you have money. Good friends are happy about your successes and sad about your setbacks.

Here's a great test: If you had casts on your arms and couldn't do anything for yourself, which of your friends would come over every day and play video games with you, help you with your homework, or hold the straw to your mouth so you could drink from a glass of lemonade? Such people would be your loyal friends.

You will evaluate and improve your friendships over time. You will learn everyone may not be suitable during certain parts of your life. They may want different things than you want. Poet Brian "Drew" Chalker warned:

"Some people are in your life for a season, and some for a reason."

That's okay! Everyone has a unique journey, but you should pursue the following:

- Be sure you do with your money what is best for you, your family, and the people you love.
- Be on the lookout for friends who only care about what you can give them.
- Make decisions with the highest character and integrity.
- Demand that those around you do the same if they want to remain in your circle.
- Always be humble and respectful to others.

We are a product of the people with whom we surround ourselves, as expressed clearly in Proverbs 13: 20:

> **"He who walks with wise people will be wise, But the companion of fools will suffer harm."**

Being around like-minded people who do the things you want to do in life is essential. "Show me your friends, and I'll show you your future."[14] So, if you have friends who are intelligent and ambitious, share this book with them so that you can help each other.

Keep in mind that success or money can lead to pride and arrogance. Remember Proverbs 16: 18,

> **"Pride comes before a fall."**

As easy as it is to rise, you can fall, left with nothing because of not being humble. Even if you fall and are humbled, you know it's just a part of the Creator's plan to teach you something. You can get back up and start again.

---

[14] (Pena, 2019)

Have self-control and discipline in your life, and always remember your higher power. Also, watch your words. Always try to speak positively. You want to speak words of encouragement to yourself and others.

You also want to know when to be quiet. Opening your mouth at the wrong time can ruin everything. It takes practice. This may seem deep, but it's so important that the "Queen of All Media" and thought leader Oprah Winfrey once said,

---

"Lots of people want to ride with you in the limo, but what you want is someone who will take the bus with you when the limo breaks down."

Do not believe anyone who tries to convince you that money guarantees happiness. There are societies with no money, but those people are happy. Indigenous groups, religious monks, and others do not have a money system. Yet people live fulfilled lives within these cultures.

Money is a tool, but it cannot bring about genuine happiness.

Some super-wealthy people − with more money than you can imagine − feel miserable. Despite their millions, singer Michael Jackson, financier Charles Schwab, entrepreneur Howard Hughes, and countless others led isolated and lonely lives.

Money does not equal happiness, health, smarts, or anything else. However, it does provide opportunities.

- If you have money, you can go to the best schools. But still not learn financial literacy.

- If you have money, you can meet people you wouldn't otherwise. But they may not include the love of your life.

- If you have money, you can buy the nicest car. But you still must drive safely to avoid an accident.

Money opens doors that poverty can't. However, you should pursue wealth only if you are willing to get it ethically and use it wisely.

The adult who gave you this book will be mad at me for telling you this. But I recommend that they figure out a way to ensure you regularly get money into your hands. You need to learn how to manage money, but you can't do that unless you have money to manage. **Yessss!!!**

But, before you get so happy about my recommendation, I don't believe that children should have money just given to them. Children should earn it. That is only a part of the money picture:

- making money,

- managing money,

- saving money,

- investing money, and

- spending money.

 Decide today — right now — that you will save at least ten percent of your money, no matter how you make it. Adopt this rule and never break it. Save ten percent of every dollar you receive from now on, and you will jump leaps and bounds ahead of most people you know.

Saving is an important lesson. If you do not listen to any other advice, listen to that. There is more to learn because you must know what to do with the ten percent you earn.

Summary

Step Two explored the concept of the wealth mindset. It cautioned that while wealth may equal abundance, it does not guarantee happiness or a sense of well-being. Money does drive accumulation. However, the accumulation of possessions does not equal abundance. Money and accumulated wealth provide powerful tools. They opened the doors to life altering opportunities. Nonetheless, these tools do not replace good, true, and faithful family and friends. With this mindset in place, your children in air should start saving and managing money now!

Step Three

Make money work for you

"Nothing will work unless you do."

- May Angelou — poet, activist, holder of the National Medal of Arts and the Presidential Medal of Freedom

No, you are not too young to make your own money!

Are you surprised to learn that you are not too young to make money? It's true. It is important for you to learn how to manage money, and you cannot do that unless you have money to manage. So, let's discover how you can earn money at almost any age.

Your parents might choose to give you an allowance. They might set up a reward system for chores you complete. Or they might help you start a venture that lets you make money. All of that is okay. But you can do things to generate money, too.

Ways Kids Make Money

There are a thousand ways or more that someone under 18 can make money. Allowances do not have to be your sole source of income. Some teenagers even own their businesses before they become adults. Try any of these ideas:

- ✓ Have a yard sale to sell toys you've outgrown.
- ✓ Do yard work for your neighbors.
- ✓ Rake leaves in the fall.
- ✓ Shovel snow in the winter.

- ✓ Provide babysitting services.
- ✓ Tutor kids in your best subject.
- ✓ Walk friendly neighborhood dogs.
- ✓ Explore gig opportunities on platforms like Twitch or Fiverr.
- ✓ Monetize your social media account as an influencer.

You may need an adult's help and permission to do such things, so talk over your plan with your parent or guardian. In a later chapter, we will cover more about what it takes to open a business. For now, just let your imagination roam free.

Think about what you might like to do. Talk to your parents, guardian, a trusted teacher, or family friend. You might discover a new product or service that no one ever thought of! Trust your own brain!

Once you start learning, you will see that you may even have a natural or creative knack for money! Very few people are naturally "bad" at handling money. What they have are bad money habits. Once better money habits replace those bad habits, people suddenly start to be good with money.

Getting a Job

Not everyone wants to start a business. That's all right. You might prefer to get a job. Young people often start in the service industry in restaurants and clothing stores. But you should always have your sights set on the job you want when you are an adult or the business you want to own.

Most people work at a job. They get up each day and go to their company to work eight or more hours. They get a paycheck at the end of the pay period (weekly, bi-weekly, or monthly). You call this **active income**. Most people earn their money as an hourly wage, while others receive a salary.

Salary = a periodic payment from an employer to an employee specified in an employment contract. It differs from piecework and hourly wages, where employers pay employees for each unit or hour completed.

There is a difference between a job and a career. A *job* is a function in a routine 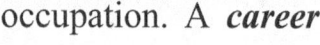  occupation. A *career* attracts you to work in a particular

field because you love the work.

Tyler the Popsicle King!

There was a boy named Tyler. His family had little money. The family couldn't buy him everything he wanted because they had to put food on the table and provide a roof over their heads. His parents had to keep the lights on and clothe Tyler's body. Tyler had seven siblings, so he didn't have any of the latest clothes or shoes. He wore clothes and shoes passed down from one brother to another.

Tyler wanted to earn more money so that he could buy a skateboard! His parents allowed him to do chores, but he tried to figure out how to turn his small allowance into more money. He went to the store one day and spent one dollar buying two popsicles at 50 cents apiece. Tyler danced and sang cheerfully, "I have popsicles! I have popsicles!!!"

Then, Tyler's friends Michael and Kim saw him and asked, "Can we buy a Popsicle from you, please?!"

Tyler said, "Sure, but I have to charge you one dollar."

Michael said, "Okay!" He gave Tyler one dollar for one pop and shared it with Kim. Kim was dancing and singing cheerfully, "I have a popsicle!"

Tyler saw how happy he had made them by selling them a popsicle. "Wow," Tyler exclaimed. "I made my whole dollar back on one Popsicle, and I made my friends happy."

Tyler ran home and asked his parents if he could do more chores. His parents said, "Yes," and Tyler worked until he saved two dollars. Tyler hurried back to the store and bought four popsicles! When Tyler got back to the neighborhood where more children waited to buy pops, he took in four dollars selling each popsicle for a dollar.

"Amazing," Tyler shouted. He bought popsicles for 50 cents and sold them for one dollar each again and again. After a while, he had so much money that his mother wanted to know where he was getting it.

He replied, "It was an **investment** I made. I took one dollar from the money I received from doing chores and turned it into three dollars!"

Tyler started reading books on money and business. He decided to keep saving so he could one day buy whatever he wanted and take care of his family. Eventually, this turned into a business that paid Tyler a steady income.

Kids can open businesses just as adults can. Nothing is stopping you from having a small, medium, or large business. Of course, you cannot sign agreements or contracts until you are eighteen. A parent or guardian will have to do that for you. But what would happen when

Tyler's friends grew older and did not want pops anymore? One afternoon, he goes out to sell his pops and only sells ten. The next day, he only sells eight. Then five the next day. He will have to be creative and think of something else he could sell. He decided to find out what went wrong with his business. What do you think Tyler should do if he still wants to sell pops? Let's see if you can think of three suggestions for him:

1. _____

   _____

2. _____

   _____

3. _____

   _____

Business = An organization providing a service or a product someone needs or wants that fills a need or makes them happy.

Running a business can be expensive. But it can also be profitable. The key is to figure out how to make more money than it costs to run the business. The remaining money is your profit, a return you can put in your pocket or reinvest into improving your business.

- Revenue = The money that comes into the business.
- Overhead = The costs for the facility, utility bills, office supplies, equipment, and inventory.
- Labor Burden = The cost to pay employees and benefits.
- Taxes = Federal, State, County, and City assessments on facilities and revenues.

Businesspeople often forget the multiple expenses involved:

- Advertising
- Legal fees
- Incorporation fees
- Cleaning fees
- Inventory
- Website and social media costs

The money left after you pay the costs is ***profit***. You want the money you make to exceed your expenses.

Tips & Tricks

Note to Parents: Do not make all the decisions for your child. Do not argue with your child about money. Help your child think about all the expenses and ways to cut costs. Your child needs your support and encouragement.

Three Types of Income

A business is not the cure-all for your financial concerns. People who have businesses work hard and long. That is why you should consider other types of income as well.

Active income = you exchange your time and work for money.

If you complete a job and get paid for it once, you receive *Active Income*. For example, if I hire you to build a fence for me, I will pay you when you finish the fence. The same happens in jobs where you earn an hourly wage or a yearly salary. The employer pays you for the work you do. If you stop working, the money stops flowing.

While I strongly advocate getting or creating a job even as a teenager, you must realize that having a job is not the quickest path to wealth. You must move into other legal sources of income that can move faster and grow bigger in time. Working ensures that you will live comfortably today. But you want your *today* money working to build you a better *tomorrow*.

For that reason, we will move into other sources of money that form the basis of wealth. Once you understand them, you can make yourself and your family wealthy long-term. Active income can grow when you get raises or a better job. But to pursue real wealth-building potential, you must move into more powerful ways of making money.

Passive income = your income does not require your labor.

Stocks, bonds, and other similar investments can make money where you do not get paid for labor.

Residual income = income comes in monthly with little **to no** effort to support it.

Residual Income rewards you for work done upfront. It takes a bunch of work at first, but then the cash rolls in month after month with little to no action on your part. For example, if you wrote a song, it could take months or years to complete it.

Once you record the song, you have no more work to do. The sales from that song will produce money for you for years to come. In fact, in the U. S., you have the right to earn money every time that song plays. That is a legacy! Having a rental property and other investments also create residual income.

Job vs. Business

When you consider working a job vs. running a business, remember that while jobs are excellent, most people do not become wealthy from their jobs alone. They either have great investments (which we will learn about soon) or they start a business. If you want to be wealthy, you will have to have control over your income. A business is the best way to do that.

You can have both a job and a business!

You don't have to choose between a job and a business. If you want to, you can have both! Each one has its benefits and drawbacks:

To have financial security, people often choose to have a job and another source of income on the side.

JOB

BENEFITS	DRAWBACKS
Steady paycheck	The business could fire you or could close at any time.
Benefits like healthcare and vacation time	Your boss tells you what to do
You can apply for as many as you want	Others compete for the job you want

BUSINESS

You love doing what you love	The business could go well sometimes and poorly at other times.
More control over your schedule	No benefits. You will have to buy health insurance out of your pocket.
You are the boss. You decided how your business runs.	Customers are not always easy to get. Once you get them, you must keep them happy.

What if I fail?

You might wonder, "But what if I fail at my business?" It's okay if you fail. Every successful person you know — every businessperson, teacher, basketball player, and even your parents — has failed at one time or another.

However, you are resilient. You'll learn valuable lessons from failure. Just pick yourself up and try again. Success rarely happens right away. There is trial and error. But I want you to know *why* you failed. If you see what went wrong, you will be better prepared. In the words of Yai Vargas, founder of *The Latinista,*

"When life hands you a difficult situation where you feel undervalued and disrespected, be bold and brave enough to know your worth."

And, speaking of failure, it is tough to fail if you will commit and work hard. You might have to start over a couple of times. But that is just part of the process. The key is to never quit!

Here is the story of someone who chose to never give up. Even though he lived over a hundred years ago, you might know his name today!

The Story of Milton S. Hershey

Born in 1857 to parents in a small farming community in the central part of Pennsylvania, Milton S. Hershey soon had his eye out for any opportunity to leave the Mennonite culture.

By 1867, Hershey's father had cut himself out of the family picture. And by 14 years old, Hershey had apprenticed with an expert confectioner in Lancaster, PA.

He would learn skills and secrets of candy making and the candy business from experts in Chicago, Denver, and New York City. He would return to Lancaster to open and build the Lancaster Caramel Company until it sold in 1900 for today's equivalent of $35 million.

Hershey would use those profits to buy land where he built The Hershey Chocolate Company and eventually produce the famous Hershey Bar and other mass-produced candies.

He and his wife would become major philanthropists, creating the Hershey Industrial School and giving it full ownership of the Hershey Chocolate Company. Their foundation would create The Hershey Museum, Hershey Gardens, Hershey Theater, and The Penn State Milton S. Hershey Medical Center.

What if my business succeeds?

Now, you might ask, "What if my business succeeds? Will I be able to manage it?" The answer is "Yes!" You may need adult help. But you will be okay.

Having started any business, you – not your parents – must run it. You will only learn how to be in charge by being in charge. As singer James Brown said, you must pay "the cost to be the boss."[15]

As noted earlier, in the United States, a person under 18 cannot make a contract — not even an oral one. However, as an adult who runs the company, you will have to do that.

Your parents will help you find an attorney to review any contract before you decide if it's good for your business. However, you don't

---

[15] (Bobbit, 1973)

have to pay hundreds of dollars per hour to have an attorney review your paperwork. Online services like www.legalshield.com offer you access to document reviews for a small monthly fee.

Learning about starting and growing your business and investing and managing your investments will prepare you for the future. Entrepreneurship is hard, so decide now that you won't give up no matter what happens. You have much to learn in a brief period. Please, have fun with this as you learn.

Don't put too much pressure on yourself. You deserve to enjoy your childhood years even if you are smart and making money. You will do great!

 Can you memorize this poem? At least try to remember the first paragraph. RECITE IT TO YOUR FAMILY WHEN YOU DO!

Don't Quit by Edgar Albert Guest

When things go wrong,
as they sometimes will,
When the road you're
trudging seems all uphill,
When the funds are low
and the debts are high,
 And you want to smile,
but you have to sigh,
When care is pressing
you down a bit,
Rest, if you must, but
don't you quit.
Life is queer with its
twists and turns,
As every one of us
sometimes learns,
And many a failure turns
about,
When he might have
won had he stuck it out;
Don't give up though the
pace seems slow
You may succeed with
another blow.

Often the goal is nearer
than,
 It seems to a faint and
faltering man,
Often the struggler has
given up,
When he might have
captured the victor's cup,
And he learned too late
when the night slipped
down,
How close he was to the
golden crown.
Success is failure turned
inside out
The silver tint of the
clouds of doubt,
And you never can tell
how close you are,
It may be near when it
seems so far,
So, stick to the fight
when you're hardest hit
It's when things seem
worst that you must not
quit.

Step Four

Invest money like the Wealthy.

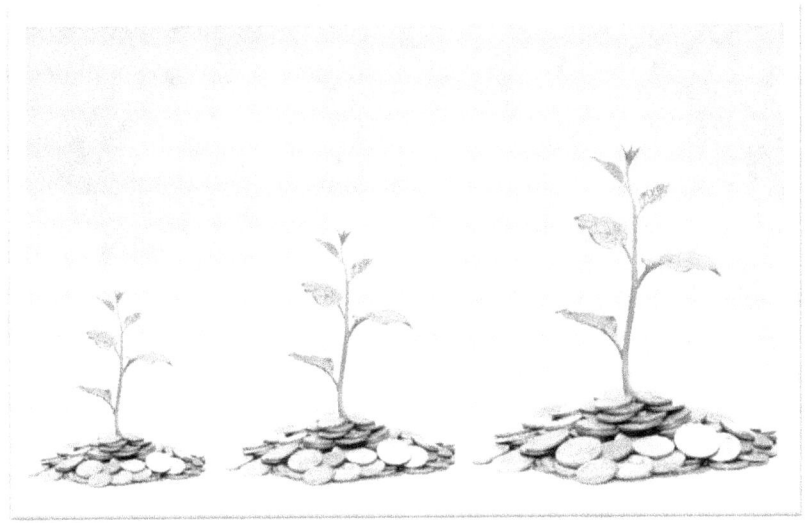

"I built a conglomerate and emerged the richest Black man in the world in 2008, but it didn't happen overnight. It took me 30 years to get to where I am today. Youths of today aspire to be like me, but they want to achieve it overnight. It's not going to work. To build a successful business, you must start small and dream big.In the journey of entrepreneurship, tenacity or purpose is supreme." Algerian billionaire Alike Dangore

Money Doesn't Grow on Trees

You have heard older people say, "Money doesn't grow on trees." They were trying to say that you must *earn* your money. But it's essential for you to know that money does grow — just not on trees. So, let's talk about how it does grow.

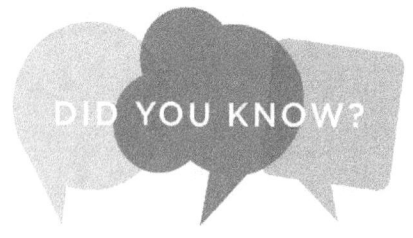

Money is just a dead piece of paper; still, it acts like a seed. If you put a seed in a pot and watch it sprout and grow, you soon find out that the seed was fully alive all along. But it had not been **activated**.

Once activated, a seed will grow into whatever nature has designed − a giant tree, a large leafy plant, a beautiful flower, or a plant-bearing fruit.

Money is made of cotton and linen − not wood-pulp paper. So, it really doesn't grow on trees!

Money is the same. When you put it to work, activating it by investing, it becomes whatever you choose. Money can grow into a larger pile of money. It can grow into luxury possessions like cars and houses. Or it can grow into lucrative investments like stocks, bitcoin, and bonds. You get to decide.

What kills a plant? Lack of moisture, sunshine, fertilizer, or too much heat, bugs, and disease. What kills money? Spending, wasting, losing, or placing it under your mattress. Money needs to be active if it is to grow.

Send your money out to work. It will come back and bring more money with it!

When you invest, you build wealth. Wealth can come from wise investments you make. Like other people, you can invest in stocks, bonds, rental properties, cryptocurrency, commodities, or  precise metals with your parents' help. Investing builds financial security and wealth because it grows your money into more money.

Financial security refers to the peace of mind you feel when you are not worried about whether your income covers your expenses. You must learn to:

1. recognize investment opportunities,
2. understand how individual investments work, and
3. how those investments might work for you.

Investing = putting money into something with the hopes of optimizing investment returns.

You should become familiar with financial terms and make them a normal part of your vocabulary and everyday life. These are the terms and types of investing you will have access to:

Stock Markets

You trade – buy, sell, and exchange – stocks, bonds, and commodities on Stock Markets. The New York Stock Exchange (NYSE) and the National Association of Securities Dealers Automated Quotations (NASDAQ) are the most prominent United States stock markets.

Stocks

Stocks = Shares of ownership of a company. When the company makes money, it awards a dividend of the profits for each share you hold.

Owning shares in a company allows you to receive benefits when the company does well. The value of shares increases if the company does well. If the company does poorly, the value of each owner's share will decrease.

You can multiply your holdings if the company succeeds. Financial analysts label those companies that routinely do well over the years as "Blue Chip" investments.

But you can lose your first investment, and whatever you made from the good fortune the company might have experienced. The company will never call you for more money if it is doing badly. But it can go out of business, making your shares worthless.

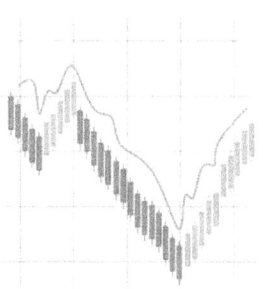

While the company stays in business, you will receive regular updates on how it is doing. You also get to vote on significant company changes and receive any special shareholder benefits the company offers. You might even receive monthly ***dividends***. If you own enough shares, stock dividends can become another excellent monthly income stream.

Do your research and work to find good companies, but the bottom line is to protect your capital or money.

Dividends = money paid to shareholders when the company is profitable.

Bonds

Bonds = government, school districts, and corporations offer bonds,

promising to repay specific amounts of money in the future.

A Bond represents a loan you have made to the bond issuer. That issuer guarantees a return for using your money to build highways and schools or expand the business. The bond promises to repay you at a specific rate, the ***coupon rate***.

When the bond comes due or ***matures***, the issuer pays back the principal invested plus the interest earned. Bonds underperform in inflationary times, but they will diversify your investment portfolio. They also carry the risk that the issuer will default.

Interest = the money earned on the money you invested.

Principal = the money you invest, hoping it will come back to you with interest.

Real Estate

People often choose to invest in more tangible assets like real estate. If you've ever played Monopoly, you already know what I mean. In Real Estate, you buy, renovate, sell, or rent out a property. You can buy as many properties and land as you can afford. There are also tax breaks for property owners and residents.

Each place you ***rent out*** can provide you with a monthly income, assuming you charge renters enough to cover your expenses and leave you a profit. If you *sell* for a higher price, it will bring in a large, one-time chunk of income.

Investing in real estate can be very **profitable.** You must put enough money into a property to fix it up to improve its value. But you should not put so much into an investment property that you cannot make a profit when selling.

If your property is the most expensive on the block, you may make it too expensive for potential buyers. But, if you are the cheapest house for sale in the area, you might cheat yourself of potential profit. There are different strategies to do this, so do your research and do the math.

Precious Metals

Precious metals = valuable elements like gold, silver, platinum, and those prized by technology.

You can invest in precious metals on stock exchanges. When the value of the dollar decreases, the values of precious metals tend to increase. But the markets in precious metals are often unstable.

Or you can buy, store, and secure tangible precious metals as a hedge against your future financial future. This assumes someone will always have an interest in purchasing your metals.

Commodities

Commodity = a product, material, or primary agricultural product bought and sold,

including copper, coffee, or pork bellies.

People invest in **commodity futures**. Investors effectively wager on what values those commodities will have in the future. Famine, disease, and global warming can wipe out investments in future commodities.

Investing Overview

The best advice is to start small and use the money you make from investing to make more. Use only a certain amount to invest. Never invest all your money in one place. This is **diversification**:

Diversification = investing in different things lowers the risk of losing all your money.

Asset

An **asset** is something a person owns with economic value. Learning about money also means understanding economics and how money works in

households, communities, cities, states, countries, and the world.

Liability

Your car represents a major investment. But it also remains a *liability*. Getting a car means you need to pay for insurance, registration, fuel, and other related charges. You pay these expenses for using your vehicle without any expectation of getting that money back.

At the same time, your car depreciates in value as soon as you drive it off the car lot. When your car develops a fault, you must spend money to fix it. When your fuel tank is empty, you spend money to fill it. Often, when you want to sell a car, you will have to sell it for less than you bought it for, or you may not be able to sell it at a reasonable price. So, you see, an *asset* puts money in your pocket, and a *liability* takes money from your pocket.

People make a financial mistake when they buy a liability, thinking it is an asset. Know the difference between what brings you money (an investment) and what takes money away from you (a liability).

Let me clarify! You can make a car an asset if you use it to offer services like Uber or Lyft. If the money you receive is more than the money you paid, your investment has value. When there is no gain, the car becomes a liability.

Sometimes, an asset can also turn into a liability if you are not careful. For instance, a house will remain an asset if people live there and pay rent. When people stop paying rent, the property turns into a liability.

Often, the things we enjoy most are liabilities. Things like skateboards, boats, and snowmobiles are liabilities, but you like them because they give you pleasure. The idea is not to abstain from buying these things but to ensure you strike a balance between your assets and liabilities. You should have enough assets that produce money before you assume liabilities.

I repeat you must **DO YOUR RESEARCH** to tell which investments are right for you!

Where will you get money to invest?

- **Ask for money instead of gifts** from parents, grandparents, godparents, aunts, and uncles. These people know the value of money. They would prefer to give you a Christmas or birthday card with cash rather than order a toy you might not like. They remember getting cash on birthdays and holidays and will be too glad to do the same for you. Then, take that money they give you and find out how you want to save or invest it.
- **Look for neighborhood opportunities.** Adults often have chores they need doing but no kids in their homes to do them. Leaves need raking. Snow needs shoveling. Grass needs to mowing.

Fences need painting. Talk to a parent about chatting with the neighbors to see what you might do.

- **Try tutoring.** Are you getting fantastic grades in a subject? Offer to help other students for a small fee. Their parents might be happy to pay you for extra help with their student.

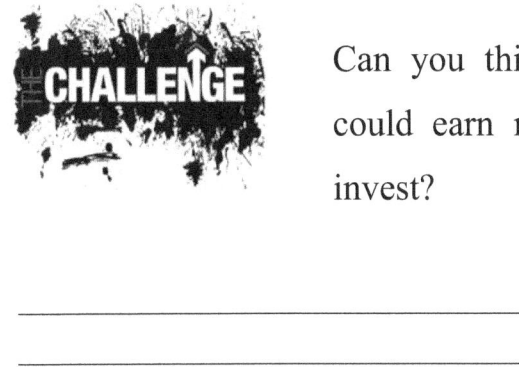 Can you think of other ways kids could earn money they can use to invest?

_____

_____

_____

_____

_____

Just be careful!!! This extra money is for your investments. Avoid spending it!

Sometimes your investments won't work out.

Investing sounds fun. It sounds like a perfect system: put money into a business, bank, or another financial goldmine, then collect your windfall of money. But there is a dark side to an investment called *risk.*

Anytime you invest your money, you must be mindful that sometimes they fail. The company you invest in could go out of business. The value of the cyber currency could fall. Economic recession may devalue your purchasing power. You may lose some or all of your money.

You buy a share of stock. But the value goes down. You panic, sell it, and the next day, it could shoot up to the moon. Stability and volatility are hard to predict in the context of a thousand things that would cause your investment to disappear.

Investing is always sort of a gamble. The significant difference is that you at least have the benefit of information about where you are investing. Go online and see what you can find about the company, its CEO, its operations and markets, and its future projections.

Do not invest more than you can afford to lose.

Always ask yourself, "How would I feel if I lost the money I'm about to invest?" If you would feel horrible, do not do it. Why? Investing is not like putting money in a bank. If you deposit $100 in the bank, the bank guarantees that your $100 will be there when you want to take it out. And the Federal government insures the deposits should the bank fail.

Investments are much riskier. When you take out your $100 deposit, there could be $200, $500, or $1000. But there is also a chance that there could only be $50, $10, or nothing. Yes, you could lose your whole $100 dollars. That is why you should make investments carefully and should only use the money you can afford to lose. Do not put all your money in investments; instead, use the profits from investments to make more money.

Investing For the Future

Another form of securing wealth is investing for the future. People will invest to cover their college costs, buy a house, or − the big one − retire. Yes, even though you are young, you should think about that day when you no longer want to work. Waiting until you are older to think about retirement could be

Investments
and Financial Planning

GLASBERGEN

"I retire on Friday and I haven't saved a dime. Here's your chance to become a legend!"

too late. And what's cool is that a small bit of money put away for retirement when you are young could grow into millions of dollars when you are 65. Imagine turning 65, and instead of having to work, you can cash a multimillion-dollar check.

That is the power of interest. When you start with even a small amount early enough, that money earns *compound interest*. That is, the interest earns interest. And that goes on and on and on until it becomes a big sum of cash. But it only works if you start early.

Embrace compound interest

Warren Buffet, the best investor of all time, started investing at the age of 50 and is now worth over $100 billion. He has said, **"My wealth has come from a combination of living in America, some lucky genes, and compound interest."**[16]

Compound interest is the addition of interest to the principal sum of a loan or deposit. It is the result of reinvesting interest rather than paying it out so that interest in the next period adds to the principal sum plus previously accumulated interest. Warren Buffet, the mega-wealthy investor, compared building wealth through interest to rolling a snowball down a hill. According to Mr. Buffet:

"I started building this little snowball at the top of a very long hill. The trick to having a very long hill is either starting young or living to be very old."[17]

[16] (Buffet)
[17] (Vega, 2022)

Compounding interest is one of the most significant mathematical discoveries of our time. Compounding makes your money work for you, generating more profits. Interest compounding grows your money exponentially! The younger you are the more time you have for interest compounding to do its job.

If your investment earned $100 interest, for example, and you reinvested it instead of taking the profit to spend you are compounding your interest. Now you will get paid dividends on that $100 also. A continual snowballing effect!

So, yes, I know retirement is the last thing on your mind. You have your whole life ahead of you. But I will tell you that the easiest way to retire wealthy is to get good at investing now.

Let's play a game!!!

The box to the right contains a short list of investing terms. Match those terms to the definitions or examples on the left. Enter the letter in the blank that makes the best match.

A. Gold, silver, platinum, and other metals or oranges, pork bellies, and coffee. B. Loaning a company or government money. C. Ownership of shares in a corporation. D. Property and rentals.	___ Bond ___ Real Estate ___ Commodities ___ Stocks

Question: What can you do *now* to become an

investor *in the future*?

_____

_____

_____

_____

Summary

This chapter covered investing. There are tons and tons of apps and bank programs designed to help kids with investing. Talk with your banker or financial advisor to help your child research the options. Kids learn that money can buy them what they want, but they need your coaching to learn how to invest in something they want. Have a monthly sit down with your kids to teach them how to check how their money is doing. Encourage them not to check their investment accounts daily. Once per month is enough!

Step Five

The Power of Budgeting, Insurance & Taxes

"A budget is telling your money where to go instead of wondering where it went."

– Dave Ramsey

Budget, Insurance & Taxes

So, now you have all this money. You know how important it is to invest. But you also have financial obligations, including insurance and taxes. How do you know how much to set aside for college, food, sneakers, video games, investing, and saving – when you have bills to pay?

The answer is a budget!

Budgeting calls for you to plan your spending. Without a budget, you may run out of money before your next paycheck or allowance. This was why Tyler decided that for him to make money, he had to budget to invest more to bring in more income.

People don't like to talk about budgets, insurance, and taxes. It's worse than talking about death and final exams! But we must discuss them. So, let's take a quick look at each.

Budget

Saving and investing will change your thinking to a positive mindset. You will begin to enjoy it and start realizing that you don't want to spend all the money you earn. You become responsible and track your money by telling it where you want it to go. You might save, invest, donate, and spend a little on things you want.

Do you think it is essential to have all the latest sneakers or pocketbooks? Some people have a thousand-dollar pocketbook and don't have a thousand dollars to put in it. Other people will park their $50,000 car in front of their $40,000 house. It's insane!

Adults fall into these spending traps and spend years struggling to get out. Don't let it happen to you! While you're young, decide what matters and focus your attention there.

When you budget, you learn not to waste money or wonder where the money went. You will always know your money goes where you want it to go. Budgeting teaches you to turn off the lights, use water and heat wisely, and spend your money prudently.

A budget helps you *live within your means*. If you do not have the money to pay for something, you should do without until you can pay for it. To be a great wealth builder, you should try to live below your means. After paying your bills, you should have money left over for saving and investing.

People who budget have their priorities straight. They budget so that they know what they can truly afford. And they put money into the places that matter rather than buying something they don't need.

Before we dive into budgets, I want to be sure you have the right attitude about it. A budget is not meant to be a prison for your money. It's your money. You worked hard to earn it. And you deserve to spend it, have fun, and buy nice things. However, a budget ensures you don't forget other expenses that are just as important. And a budget makes sure that you remember to save and invest.

With a budget, you use a spreadsheet or app to look at the money you expect to make and what you plan to do with it. That way, you don't miss your priorities. Figure 3 following illustrates the budget process.

Figure 3: The Budget Process

You begin your budget by setting clear goals and expectations: what you ***want to spend*** money on, what ***you must spend***, and how much ***you want to set aside***. Figure 4 on the following page illustrates a hypothetical budget.

As you budget, you discover the facts about your spending using your bank and credit card records. Then you distribute your income to show how the data will meet or fail your goals.

Each week or month, you will check your spending habits to see what works and does not work for you before you adjust the budget to make up for the differences.

Figure 4: A Hypothetical Monthly Budget*

Income		Expenses		Percent Budgeted
$3810		$3780		
Pay	$3,200	Rent	$1,000	
Gig	$500	Car	$400	
Investment	$100	Utilities	$150	
Aunt Sally	$10	Internet	$100	50%
		Gas	$100	
		Loans	$300	
		Groceries	$300	
		Personal	$100	
		Eating Out	$200	50%
		Entertainment	$200	
		Clothing	$150	20%
		Cable TV	$30	
		Savings	$750	

*These figures may not reflect inflation or your current experience with income or spending. But they do illustrate an effort to bring income and spending into line.

A monthly budget must also include spending for certain necessary expenses, including the following:

Car Insurance

You must never drive any car without insurance. Every month you pay a certain amount of money called a **premium**. This protects you and your auto investment if there is an unfortunate accident, and it might keep other drivers from suing you if you caused the wreck.

Health insurance

It doesn't matter how much money you have if you do not feel well. Your health is your number one commodity. So be sure to keep your health insurance current despite its expense. Hopefully, your employer will share the cost.

Home Insurance

You also need homeowner's or renter's insurance. If you have insurance and something goes wrong – and things will go wrong, the insurance company pays to fix things. In return for your premium, the insurance company promises to pay a certain amount to cover expenses if you experience a catastrophic event listed in your policy.

Life insurance

Adults should ensure their family against the final expenses of funeral and burial. A life insurance policy, secured early in life, will cost much less than later. If anyone relies on your income, you need life insurance.

Life Insurance proceeds can also be a form of **generational wealth** if you take it out early enough. Get a large policy and leave a significant amount for each beneficiary heir.

Some people feel they can invest the premiums better, using other investments and making more money. However, Whole Life Insurance Policies provide investment guarantees you can accumulate or cash in. It's up to you. I suggest you weigh your options and shop around.

The question you need to answer is, "If I were to die today, would those I support be able to take care of themselves?" If the answer is "No," then you need life insurance. Just keep the amount of the policy a secret and in a will filed with a lawyer.

Taxes

At the end of the year, you must know how to file and pay taxes to the government. Make sure you keep all paperwork of your expenses throughout the year. Even the smallest expense can help you reduce your taxes.

Kids usually don't pay taxes unless they earn over a certain amount. What amount? If you make more than $599, an employer will present a Form 1099. The IRS will expect you to report this form's earnings. You may have to pay taxes on high earnings – even if you are still a kid. **You should be aware of tax advantages for business owners and investors.** Some of the things are that you get to write off expenses. This will lower the amount of money you have to pay. Some of that you can write off as a business owner are: Car expenses and mileage—office expenses, rent, utilities, health insurance premiums, phone bills, continuing education, etc. It would help if you spoke to your accountant about all the advantages you are entitled to. Tax advantages for investors refer to favorable tax status held by certain qualified investments, accounts, or other financial vehicles. Common examples include municipal bonds, 401ks or 403b accounts, 529 plans, and certain types of partnerships. Again, see your financial expert or advisor for the complete list.

These responsibilities and the fun stuff make up your financial bank of knowledge. Take it seriously. When you are an adult, you will be glad you did. Good money management saves you headaches and heartaches as an adult. Consider the words of entrepreneur and music production mogul Russell Simmons.

> *"I don't think it is an exaggeration to say that financial literacy, economic empowerment, and wealth building is going to be the last leg of the civil rights movement. Because one step toward financial literacy takes you two steps toward personal empowerment."*

Summary

Kids love helping their parents work on the family budget. This teaches children how to accept personal responsibility as we show them good money management. We teach children that they have a say in their financial future and have more control as they grow older. Whether you have a lot of money or not, you can teach your children the importance of budgeting as a parent or educator. These habits will stay with them for a lifetime. Kids with a strong financial education have more options!

Step Six

All About Credit

"*If you dare to struggle, you dare to win.
If you dare not struggle, then you don't
deserve to win.*"

— *Fred Hampton – antiracist, anti-classist Rainbow
Coalition*

Be very careful about credit!

Sometimes, we can use other people's money to invest – if we have good credit.

Credit = money extended to you by lenders based on your record paying other creditors.

You must be careful about credit. "Credit" refers to borrowing money, although you may never see the money. For example, you might have a credit card that allows you to spend up to $500. The bank doesn't send you $500. Instead, it issues you a credit card that lets merchants know that the bank will pay for anything you buy up to that $500 limit.

People like having access to purchasing power. It can come in handy for emergencies when you're short of cash. But you must remember you will get a bill from the bank at the end of the month listing everything you bought – plus interest and finance charges. Credit cards also often come with an annual fee.

Interest = The amount you must pay a bank or other lender for the privilege of using their money.

When you get a credit card bill, you have three choices:

1. Pay it in full,

2. Pay the smallest amount they ask for and the rest later, and

3. Don't pay, letting your account go into a **delinquent** status.

The bank will report your payment habit to credit bureaus. If you pay your bills on time and in full, they will report that you are an **excellent risk** because you pay all your bills before their due dates. They will report that you are a **good risk** if you pay the minimum. If you don't pay, they will report that you are an **unsafe risk** because you don't pay on time or at all. Ask your parents if you can help with paying the bills. This will give you a good idea of what's paid out and what balance remains.

This "report" I keep mentioning is your *Credit Report*, an essential piece of your financial picture. Your credit report will tell others if you have financial integrity.

Credit Report = a list of all your debts and how you have paid them over the last seven to twelve years.

Remember this: ***don't borrow the money you can't pay back***! You want to pay back any debt on time. If you don't, it will hurt you financially for years to come. The credit report affects your ability to buy a car or secure a mortgage. What's worse, the next time you want to borrow, the charge for borrowing will be much higher.

Banks, retail stores, and gasoline companies will assault you with applications while your credit is good. But you must resist multiplying your credit cards. You might feel you can buy anything, but the debt will catch up.

Credit card vendors will offer low-interest rates. Still, it would be best to search their offer for the **Annual Percentage Rate (APR)** to understand what the credit will cost you.

For example

Suppose you go to your favorite clothing store and buy a shirt for $29.00. If you have a credit card, you can swipe it to let the store know your credit card company will pay the bill. At the end of the month, the credit card company will bill you for $29.00.

However, they will give you the choice of paying the whole balance or a part. If you choose to pay something other than the entire balance, they will charge you interest on the amount you don't pay.

If you are late, they will charge you a late fee *and* report to the credit bureau that you paid late. Such reports lower your credit score. Now you must pay the late fee plus the cost of the shirt. You could have saved and invested the money you paid in interest.

Every penny counts. Would you rather have a million dollars or a penny doubled every day for 30 days? Let me show you why the penny is better in Figure 6.

Figure 6: A Penny Doubled Every Day

Day	Balance	Day	Balance	Day	Balance
1	$0.01	11	$10.24	21	$10,485. 76
2	$0.02	12	$20.48	22	$20,971.52
3	$0.04	13	$40.96	23	$41,943.04
4	$0.08	14	$81.92	24	$83,886.08
5	$0.16	15	$163.84	25	$167.772.16
6	$0.32	16	$327.68	26	$335,544.32

7	$0.64	17	$655.36	27	$671,088.64
8	$1.28	18	$1,310.72	28	$1,342,177.28
9	$2,56	19	$2,621.44	29	$2,684,354.58
10	$5.12	20	$5,242.88	30	$4,368,709.12

That above shows you that every penny counts! With credit, you want to pay on time because your integrity is on the line. Your credit reflects how well you keep your promises.

Let's look again at Tyler, our popsicle king. Our popsicle entrepreneur sells popsicles for one dollar a piece. On another day, Noah came to Tyler after school. He said, "Hey Tyler, I would like a Popsicle today, but I won't get money from chores around the house until next Saturday."

Tyler replied, "I can give you a pop today on credit, but instead of the one dollar they usually cost, I will have to charge you extra."

"Why do you have to charge me extra?" Noah asked.

"It's because I'm giving you the privilege of eating the popsicle today in exchange for your promise to pay me next Saturday."

Credit is an agreement in which a person (borrower) receives something of value from someone (lender) to pay back the money in the future with interest. Credit allows you to have something just for signing paperwork that says you will agree to pay for it later. This is how credit works.

The big problem with credit is that you must use it with discipline. If Noah is not careful, he can use credit to buy more things the next day, the next day, and the next day. By the time he gets his allowance next Saturday, Noah may find that he owes more people than he can afford to pay. He is "overextended.'

Overextended = you owe more each month in credit than you can afford to pay.

The financial system will assign you a credit FICO (Fair Isaac Corporation) score as you build your economic life. Three main Credit Bureaus support the FICO: **Experian®, TransUnion®, and Equifax®**.

Regulations allow you to **check your credit for free** online or go to www.annualcreditreport.com. Companies usually average the scores at these credit bureaus to decide where your credit stands. Or they take the middle score. For example, the Experian score is 750; the Equifax score is 790, and the Transunion score is 760. Companies checking your credit rating would go with the 760 score before they authorize your loan.

Sometimes things get on your report by mistake or through fraudulent activity. You want to report this to the bureaus at once! It makes sense to order the report from one bureau at a time, three times per year. For example, you can order from Experian in January, Transunion in June, and Equifax in September. That way, you can keep an eye on your reports to ensure everything is correct during the year.

Apps like www.creditkarma.com/ and www.freecreditreport.com allow you to check your credit daily. Stay on top of your credit because companies where you try to buy big-ticket items will check that credit report and score to see if you are a good risk.

Before companies or banks loan you money, they check with the credit bureau. Lenders consider an 850-score perfect, but they consider anything score over 750 excellent. You will get the loan at a reasonable interest rate if the score is high enough. Lenders may approve your loan at a higher interest rate if your credit is good or fair. But they will deny the loan if your credit is poor or bad. Loan sharks will lend you money with a bad credit rating, but they will charge you a fortune in interest.

America has built its economy on people borrowing money for houses, cars, businesses, and other things. When you go to buy a home, the house may cost $250,000. Most people don't have that kind of money, so they must go to a bank to borrow it.

The bank will give you a mortgage payment plan, like paying rent, except you keep the property at the end of your mortgage payments. With rent, you are paying to lease or rent to live somewhere, and then you will have to move at the end of the agreed-upon lease or rental period. Mortgages are 15-to-30-year loans to buy, so the bank must know they can trust you for that long.

The interest rate you will pay on the mortgage depends on your credit score and the current interest rates set by the Federal Reserve Bank. You have at least a 650-credit score before a lender will offer a mortgage loan.

Of course, kids don't have credit scores and can't borrow money from banks because they can only enter a contract once they are 18. But parents with good credit can put children on their credit cards as **"authorized users."** That will give you a head start in the credit world.

Building your credit is important and should start as soon as you are old enough. Only join an adult's credit card as an "authorized user" if the primary user has a good credit record. That credit score will be your credit score.

Parents: Do not put your bills in your kids' names, ruining their credit, and don't let people put their bills in yours. It takes seven years for bad debt to fall off your credit score, and you do not want that burden on your children's bad debt.

What happens if you cannot pay?

Sometimes people experience traumatic circumstances that affect their ability to pay their bills. A major illness, the loss of a job, or a global pandemic can significantly affect your ability to pay bills.

But remember what we talked about previously. It would help if you positioned yourself to have the savings necessary to get you through the tough times.

Communication with your creditors is critical. Call them and explain your circumstances; they can figure out a plan to help. They may delay payments. If a service rep says they cannot help you, always ask to speak to a manager. If the manager cannot help you, ask to talk to her boss. Keep trying until you get results. Remember the little engine that thought he could climb that mountain! Keep trying.

Creditors will call your house daily to hound you for the money you owe them. They will send multiple bills to your home. They may sue you in court. They may even ***garnish*** your wages. If you have a poor credit rating, they can force your employer to pay them first and give you what's left over. They will **repossess** your car if you buy it on credit and don't pay.

With a mortgage, the bank holds the deed of ownership for your house until you pay them back. Sadly, if you don't pay, they *evict* you, kicking you out of the house, and selling it to someone else to recoup their money. They will transfer the deed to the new owner. Worse, you will not get the money back that you already spent on the property.

Banks don't want to take your home from you, but they are in the business of making money. The way they make money is to charge you interest on the money you borrowed. If you don't pay, they want to at least get back the money they loaned you.

Does all of this seem harsh? People might someday borrow from you and refuse to pay you back. They might make excuses because they cannot pay you back, like, "The dog ate my money" or "I don't remember borrowing from you." Perhaps this has already happened to you. How does it make you feel? Angry? Frustrated? You'll find answers in the words of Vernon Brundage, Jr., basketball star, author, and Founder and Executive Director of investED Enrichment Services, Inc., a non-profit committed to fostering life skills among underserved youth:

***Excuses are tools of the incompetent.
They build monuments of
nothingness. Those who choose to
use them seldom amount to
anything.***

Don't Make Excuses

Keeping your word is part of the social contract we make with each other. We expect that people are going to do what they say. You must honor your promises to build trust with companies, banks, and others. Debt can be an addictive trap for people who aren't careful and responsible. Once you mess it up, it's hard to restore confidence.

Debt = the sum of money you owe. You owe a debt if

you agree to give

or do something for someone else.

Factors Affecting Credit Score

The following terms may help you understand how credit bureaus determine your credit score and the different types of debt:

- **Secured Debt** needs collateral. The borrower must supply a property or asset that covers the debt. Examples of collateral include vehicles and houses. Once the debtor (you) defaults (doesn't pay), the lender can repossess the asset.

- **Unsecured Debt** does not need collateral as security. Because there is no collateral, the lender depends on the borrower's credit profile as the primary determining factor in approving or denying loans. Examples include student loans and retail store accounts. A FICO® score weighs and integrates these five factors. Each factor may include several elements:

    1. Payment Record (35%)
    2. Amount Owed (30%)
    3. Length of Credit History (15%)
    4. New Credit (10%)
    5. **Credit Mix (10%)**

- **Debt usage** refers to the frequency with which you incur debt. The amount you owe is what can hurt you here. Keep your debt below 30%. If you have a credit card with a $1,000 credit limit, you should have at most $300 on that card. Also, you should use less than 30% of your total available credit across all sources.

- **Length of credit history** looks at how long you have had credit. You need to set up good credit early. You may become authorized users on your parent's credit cards to show good credit. You must show people early that you will pay them back to save money in the future on interest rates for purchases like cars or houses.

- **Credit mix** considers the diversity in your portfolio of credit accounts. Lenders prefer to see a variety of credit accounts. For example, they would like to see only some of your debt tied up in retail store accounts.

- **New Credit** factors include the number of credit accounts you've recently opened or applied for and the number of inquiries lenders make when you apply for credit. Frequent credit inquiries suggest your borrowing is unstable.

- **Revolving credit accounts** are usually offered by large retail stores. These accounts only require you to pay a minimum amount of your balance each month. If you pay the minimum, the remaining balance rolls into the next month, subject to compounding interest charges.

- **Installment accounts** require you to pay a fixed sum each month based on factors such as the total amount borrowed, the term of the loan, and the established interest rate. Mortgages, auto loans, and personal loans are installment accounts.

- **Non-Installment/service credit or open accounts** allow the borrower to pay later for service, membership, or subscription. Payment is due the month following the service, and unpaid balances will incur a fee, interest, or penalty charge. Continued non-payment will result in service cancellation and a report to the credit bureau. Cell phones, gas and electricity, water, and garbage services fall in this category. These companies often encourage automatic payments from your bank account.

How Credit Helps

Credit also can work in your favor. When you lend money to someone, you can check their credit score to decide if it's a good idea. While most people who loan money to friends and family don't bother checking credit, others are wise and ask for a contract and collateral.

Tips & Tricks

Contract: An agreement − oral or written − concerning work, employment, sales, or money enforceable by law.

Collateral: An asset pledged as security for repayment of a loan and given up in the event of a default.

You must Maintain a Positive Credit Score.

Once you damage your credit, it can take years to recover and get back on track. On the other hand, people who have good credit get lots of perks!

- People with good credit pay less for the insurance they must have as adults.

- People with good credit pay lower interest rates on loans and credit cards.

- Certain jobs require good credit.

- The better your credit, the better your deal when you borrow.

How to Improve Your Credit Score

These six steps will improve your credit score:

1.   Pay your bills on time.

2.   Pay off debt and keep debt low

3.   Pay bills early and consistently.

4.   Avoid closing a credit card account.

If you want to stop using a specific credit card, you should stop using it rather than closing the account. Depending on the age and credit limit of the card, closing the credit card account can hurt your credit score.

5.   Avoid inquiries on your account. Employers, financial institutions, credit card companies, courts, and individuals may inquire about your creditworthiness.

- **Hard Inquiries**, such as when you apply for a credit card, lower your credit score by as much as 10 points and take 2 years to come off your report. Ten points may not sound like much, but they can have an influence in the world of credit.

- **Soft Inquiries** include checks you make on your credit status or those caused by lenders who check to see if you meet their pre-approval requirements. Soft Inquiries only affect your credit a little.

If you see an inquiry on a report that is not yours, you can dispute it and try to get it removed.

Figure out the kind of inquiry when someone wants to check your credit. For instance, when shopping for a mortgage, several investigations should show up as a single inquiry if they occur within 45 days. Creditors should realize you are searching for a mortgage—same thing for a car. Try to go shopping knowing your credit score in advance so you can get estimates before they make a hard inquiry.

If you have questions, research or get credit counseling from free credit service companies. If you mess up your credit standing, you may have to hire a reputable service to help you out.

To pay off credit cards, you must pay the smallest debt first. That gives you a sense of accomplishment. Then you move on, paying each card until they are all paid off! Or you can first focus on paying down and off the card with the highest APR rate.

Summary

Once again, parents should lead by example. If your credit is out of order, you are less likely to help your child. It is shockingly easy to clean up your credit period it just takes time and discipline. Communicate with your creditors. All creditors have a deferment or forgiveness plan. But lack of communication will lead to late fees, repossessions, foreclosures, judgments, write offs, and collections. Once an account reaches the creditors collection department, getting it off your credit report is nasty business. The worst strategy is to ignore your creditors and let them take matters into their own hands. For old debts, dispute anything you don't recognize or accept. People have found that those items drop off the credit report with a simple letter to the credit bureaus. Your good credit can help your child establish good credit period children can help pay your bills, giving them practice and an understanding of credit and obligations to pay.

Step Seven
Be A Producer

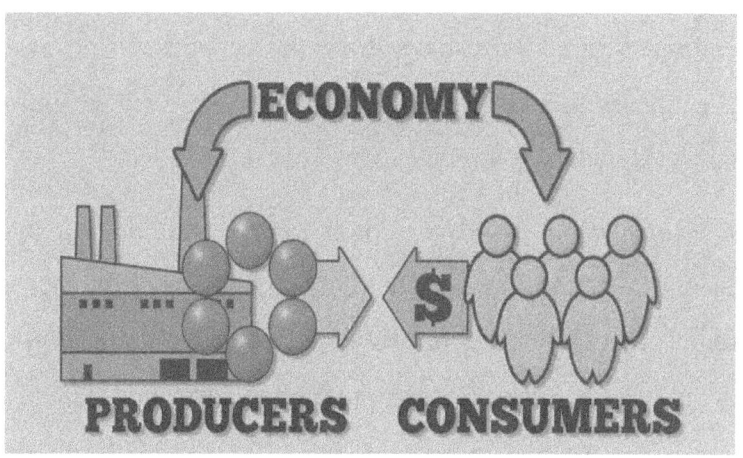

All production is for the purpose of ultimately satisfying a consumer.

— John Maynard Keynes, Nobel Prize winner in Economics

The Materialism Mindset

Economy refers to "the wealth and resources of a country or region, especially in the production and consumption of goods and services."[18]

Producers and **Consumers** drive the economy. And a strong, stable economy depends on the balance between vendors and purchasers. However, people have become materialistic.

The *Materialism Mindset* addicts people into buying material possessions. While possessions are not bad in themselves, the issue is that most possessions are *liabilities* – not *assets*. **Liabilities** take money out of your pocket. *Assets* put money into your pocket.

Society has programmed people since childhood, making them subconscious but consistent consumers. They only buy, buy, buy! Every day, you see advertisements with messages that convince you to buy things you do not need.

People do not multiply possessions because they make more money or have more wages but because they can *easily access bad debt*. There is **good debt**, where you invest in mortgages or things that bring in more income. But **bad debt** results from spending on things you do not need, a habit that will not increase your wealth. Debt

---

[18] (Mariotti & Glackin, 2014)

enslaves people, buying more stuff they do not need in an economy where it is much easier to borrow money.

Being an excessive, wasteful consumer of things enslaves you. It destroys your liberty, removes your peace of mind, and accumulates unnecessary purchases. It can affect your well-being and interactions with others. When you buy things you cannot afford, you become increasingly indebted to others and dig yourself into financial misery.

Producer versus Consumer

How do you understand and manage your finances with production and consumption? First, let's define *producer* and *consumer*.

- A **producer** creates or makes the products and services others buy or consume. For example, Nike makes sneakers.

- A **consumer** buys the things that producers create. For example, people who play sports need to buy sneakers. They don't make sneakers. They buy them from people who do.

We all function as consumers and producers at one time or another. Adam Smith, the 18th-century pioneer in Economics and author of the earth-shaking *The Wealth of Nations*, wrote:

> *Consumption is the sole end and purpose of all production, and the interest of the producer ought to be attended to only so far as it may be necessary for promoting that of the consumer.*

A Consumer Mindset

Consumers live by using things produced by others. It's okay to be a consumer. Consumption drives the economy. We must buy things to sustain our lives. The global economy depends on consumers. So, be sure you are an integral part of this community of people who make the world run. Some people become addicted to maximizing their debt by accumulating things, a behavior shaped by materialism. Their psychology tells them that abundance equals wealth, prestige, and celebrity. However, too many live by incurring debt and living paycheck to paycheck.

A Producer Mindset

Producers focus on solving problems and creating products and services through which money can flow to consumers. Producers cultivate their thinking and skills to create innovations, take entrepreneurial risks, and add value to people's lives. If you think like a producer, you will become one. You might think like the rapper, entrepreneur, and philanthropist Sean "Diddy" Combs, who said,

"What you might not realize, what I think a lot of people don't know, is that from the get-go, when I started my first job, I was only 12 years old. I was a paper boy. And the way I got the job was really through my entrepreneurial spirit, which is something I got from my mother."

You are whom you think you are. For instance, members of marginalized communities have proven histories as producers:

- Garret Morgan, the son of enslaved people, created the traffic light.

- At 17 years old, Alissa Chavez patented a device that could prevent babies and children left alone in cars from dying of heat strokes.

- Dr. Gladys West created the GPS (Global Positioning System).

- Flossie Wong-Staal, Ph.D., cloned HIV (human immunodeficiency virus), a work that improved the understanding of the cause of AIDS (acquired immunodeficiency syndrome).

- Thomas David Petit, a descendant of the Chippewa, invented the ad hoc wireless network behind cell phone networks.

We could also include producers like Roberto Clemente, Jackie Robinson, Michael Jordan, Kristi Yamaguchi, Greg Louganis, and other athletes, entertainers, and thinkers who have improved the lives of others.

Innovation is an inherent human trait.

We all can produce something at one time or another. Children love creating, from using paper sheets to building blocks. We all can birth innovative ideas, develop innovative ways to solve problems, offer excellent services, provide value, and produce different valuable products.

Your ability to produce is a function of your potential and gifts. Of course, everyone won't be an entrepreneur, but anyone can be an investor, business owner, freelancer, marketer, or partner. These are some of the ways people produce.

The way to break free from the consumer mentality is to start thinking of ways to produce and create things the world might want. With a mind open to possibilities, you'll see opportunities around you. It's not about where you are; it's about how you think. Life becomes easier when you move from thinking like a consumer to thinking like a producer.

When you think of ways to make more money or invest, you switch to the producer mentality. Eventually, you will begin to get ideas, see opportunities, and grow as a producer. You will create products and services and contribute values. This is the financial shift you need. The truth is producers get wealthy, and compulsive frivolous consumers become poor. This is because consumers pay the producers for their goods and services.

Investors are Producers

Investors are producers. Even though they don't make things, investors provide the money that ensures things get made. Again, an investor puts money into a business, real estate, stock, or something else, hoping there will be profit or interest. Investment management firms and banks use our money to develop businesses, buy properties, engage in currency exchange, etc. We can use professional firms or do it ourselves to make more money to care for ourselves and our families.

Producers invest in businesses that sell things or make things that they sell. To be wealthy and in control of your life, you must be a producer.

You can produce a service for people or sell them things. Anything that you do that pays an income makes you a producer.

You should develop a mindset for creating more than one income stream toward wealth. It will give you the power to influence your community. You should build up wealth and pass the mentality and the businesses, as well as the lessons on being a producer, to your families for generations to come.

 **What could you produce that others might find helpful?**

What favorite activities do you have that could be money-making opportunities?

_____

_____

_____

How can you improve that activity to make it more enjoyable for you and others and, at the same time, make something people might buy?

_____

_____

_____

Is there something you could teach people or a service you can offer that would be valuable to others?

_____

_____

_____

Invest Time to Learn About Your World

As a producer, you must invest time to learn more about your world and what people need that they don't have. It takes time, but it has rewards.

People who create things always think about their customers. They ask themselves what problems they could solve by making something great.

One young girl heard her parents complaining about how greasy the bacon was after frying. She watched as her parents dabbed off the oil from the grease when they pulled it from the oven, frying pan, or microwave. This girl decided to make a rack to lay the bacon over. The oil dripped into a pan below, leaving a perfectly cooked row of bacon above. It sold like hotcakes, and this girl made millions.

What would help your family or other families? Have you ever said, "Why isn't there an easier way?"

The big lesson here is not to think of money as something to spend, spend, spend. But to think of ways to get money flowing in instead of flowing out.

The most crucial lesson in this chapter is that you learn to think productively and produce goods or services. Every wealthy person is a producer of something. The poor keep buying things that make them spend more money, but the rich buy things that make them make more money.

Step Eight

Learn the Art of Negotiating

"At the bottom of education, at the bottom of politics, even at the bottom of religion, there must be for our race economic independence."

— *Booker T. Washington, educator, author, and advisor to Presidents*

Life is one big yard sale

Many people struggle with money because they pay the full price for everything! However, ***almost everything*** is negotiable. Life is one big yard sale. Nine times out of ten, you'll find the seller willing to talk price.

Negotiation is an undeniably crucial aspect of a successful business. Negotiating a good deal is not always easy, but you must develop the skill. Modern business professionals must master the critical skill of negotiating.

People often take things personally when it comes to negotiation because they do not understand. You should not always accept the price of products or services (particularly big-ticket items) as final. Price is determined by what the customer is willing to pay.

Negotiation may not seem comfortable, but it gets easier once you start doing it. You cannot overemphasize the value of bargaining – cannot. Negotiation saves you hundreds of thousands of dollars in a lifetime.

Seven Critical Tips on Negotiating

When buying big-ticket items like a car, you should ask questions. These seven questions, outlined on www.Zenbusiness.com[19], offer a guide:

1. **Would you explain the reasons for your price?**

   You must find the reasoning behind the price. Once you know the seller's thinking, you can develop a team approach where you both get what you want.

2. **Is there any reason you can't lower the price?**

   Sometimes you discover that the other party rejects your offer for no legitimate reason or needs to think it over. Such people make excuses for why they can't do something or shoot down an idea with short-sighted objections. When you ask questions this way, the other party often needs help producing legitimate reasons that effectively dismiss your offer.

3. **Why do you think this is a *fair* and *reasonable* price?**

   "Fair" implies a "balance of conflicting ideas" about the price. "Reasonable" means "not extreme or excessive." So, establishing a *fair* and *reasonable* understanding should level the playing field. You can determine an offer's reasonableness with research into

---

[19] (Lewis-Fernandez, 2020)

comparable product pricing. Suppose the seller's price exceeds the pricing at similar area stores. In that case, you will have the leverage to press the seller to define and defend the reasonableness of their price position.

4. Why is that point or provision so important?

Understanding the significance of a specific price point will help you adjust your position. The other side's response to this question will help you to fine-tune your negotiation strategy. Understanding, acknowledging, and confirming the significance of the seller's position enables you to recalibrate your approach and cultivates a team affinity, building a level of trust at a faster pace. Fair and reasonable sellers will appreciate that you care about what is important to them and are more willing to negotiate.

5. What part of my proposal gives you the most concern?

When you break an offer down into individual elements, it makes it easier to understand things. Ask the other person what most concerns them about your offer.

6. What documentation or proof do you have to validate your position?

"If it sounds too good to be true, it probably is." So, "Trust but verify!" The negotiation should focus on something other than likes or dislikes when you could have facts at hand. When buying a car, for example, you can arm yourself with documentation from the web. The manufacturer's website will list product specifics. But you will also find pricing recommendations at Edmunds.com or Kelly Blue Book.

7. What else should I know?

Open-ended questions force the other person to talk more. The more they talk, the more information you get. That information may reveal something you did not know. It might influence your thinking, what you are looking for, or the best strategy to pursue. In any negotiation, however large or small, direct communication with open-ended questions is vital. People often don't ask such questions because they fear rejection or how they will be perceived. Such concerns remind me of the words of Rabbi Noah Weinberg, the New York-born founder of Aish HaTorah Institutes throughout the world:

"People often avoid making decisions out of fear of making a mistake. The failure to make decisions is one of life's biggest mistakes."

Other things to think about:

- Never feel like you must have something. Don't be anxious about anything. Always be willing to compromise on what you buy.
- Delay your purchase until the price and terms are acceptable.
- Use the internet to discover pricing and discounts.

Only pay what you can afford! If you don't have the money, control your impulse to buy and purchase it later. Don't fall back on credit just to get it now. You won't negotiate if you can whip out a credit card and pay the price charged.

Ways you can negotiate better include:

- **Pay cash for a better deal.** Sellers pay all significant fees associated with accepting credit cards from customers. Many stores will give you a discount if you pay cash.

- **Ask lots of questions**. Just remember that the salesperson will ask questions to get you to buy. Do the reverse. Ask them a lot of questions to get them to lower the price.

- **Don't fall in love**. The best negotiators are the ones who aren't afraid to walk away. If you buy a car and fall in love with one specific vehicle, the salesperson will have you right where they want you. Make sure the salesperson knows you have alternatives, and they will give you a better price. Wait to buy until you've left the showroom at least a couple of times. You can bet the salesperson will come after you with one final better deal!

- **Don't be afraid to use the word no**. Your "NO" will save you from doing things you don't want to do. It is so freeing.

- **Don't ever be afraid to ask for the money owed to you!** Refunds, loans, credits, discounts, and more belong to you.

Practice these principles because saying "NO" and
"asking for your money"
doesn't come easy for some people.

Step Nine
Do What You Love & Help Whom You Can

I DON'T HAVE A BAD ATTITUDE SIR. I ALREADY TOLD YOU THAT WE HAVE OUTSOURCED ALL NON-ESSENTIAL TASKS LIKE BEING EMPATHETIC AND COURTEOUS. SO WE CAN FOCUS ON WHAT'S REALLY IMPORTANT.

"Get involved with things that you love and be sure to have a standard and integrity with what you're doing."

- JAY Z (Sean Corey Carter), entrepreneur, hip-hop artist, and thought leader

"If you do what you love, you'll never work a day in your life."

— Marc Anthony, singer, songwriter, and actor

Life is great when you do what you love.

In my opinion, you will not find true financial fulfillment if you don't love what you do −even if no one paid you.

It doesn't matter how old you are. Being wealthy or rich has nothing to do with your age. Video games, for example, may be liabilities with no financial return from them. However, if you love video games, you can find a way to make the things you love to turn a profit for you. For example, you might decide to rent out your games, cartoons, and books to your friends to make money off your assets. Finding and doing what you love allows you to do things with ease while others struggle to find their way.

You also want to ***do something for which you have natural gifts***. You may have a passion for art, but your natural gift for computers may earn you the money to enjoy your passion for art! Passion refers to the thing that you love to do even at your lowest moments.

You know it's a passion because you always have an enthusiastic attitude toward it. You don't get tired, you always want to try new things, and you can channel that energy into making it stand out.

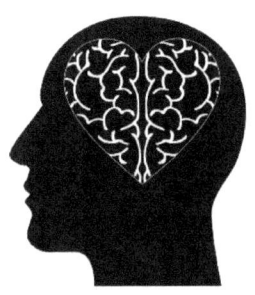 The passion for what you do is a productivity booster. It increases your performance. You become more optimistic and motivated, learning fast, making fewer mistakes, and producing smarter decisions.

- Jenna loves to cook! It's easy and fun for her because she loves it and makes money at it. Jenna tries out new recipes, which come out great with little guidance. She caters to events and has started a food blog many people visit.

- David likes to fix things. He is handy at tasks around the house. David opened his shop; now David can't stop. He opened two more stores, and they succeeded. David does what he likes best, so it's fun for him.

- Deja loves doing hair. She opened a hair salon; now, Deja does hair from morning to night! She opened a bigger store and now has a line of customers that goes out the door!

- Neesh fixes people's credit, so she started her credit repair business. But Neesh also has income from owning real estate, stocks, and other things.

- Dupree loves cars. He started washing cars as a business. He saved the money he made from washing cars and invested it back into the company, which grew into multiple car wash locations.

- Chris and John taught themselves about stocks and options, then started teaching others and turned it into a business.

127

- When you do what you love, and it's your passion, it makes work easier.

Always try to make the customer happy!

The customer is usually always right because it's their experience of how they feel − even if they are wrong in your eyes. Sometimes you have to agree to disagree with clients. If you keep your customers happy, they will tell a friend about your business. If they don't get what they want, you can only hope they let you know so you can fix things to the best of your ability. However, in this age of social media, unhappy customers quickly share their disappointment with others. Consider the words of Maya Angelou, the American poet, actress, and Civil Rights activist who holds the Presidential Medal of Freedom:

A person may forget what you say but will never forget how you made them feel.[20]

Granted, you will not be able to make everyone happy. Some people have other things going on in their life and will try to bring their negativity into your space. Do what you can for them, let it go, and move on.

---

[20] (Gallo, 2014)

You need a thick skin in business and as an entrepreneur. You cannot let every little thing bother you. Things worth having don't come easy in life, and things that come too easy are seldom worth having.

Everyone has a gift, something that comes naturally to them and that they do well with little effort. We all have unique skills and superpowers. Still, you must work at it, but that's your gift if it comes easier for you than others. Sometimes, you may have to try several things before you find your passion.

Setting Goals

Setting goals is fun. Set goals for your money. How much would you like to make in the next three months? What would you like to spend? How much do you want to invest?

Goals need timelines. You must set down specific dates when planning. More importantly, you must **write your plan down**; otherwise, you only have a wish list. Write down each step to achieve your goals, and your wildest dreams can come true! If you start by finding your passion, you can set clear goals about how far you want to go in that field and what you want to accomplish. But you must have a plan.

Always have a plan and write it down. **Write it down! Write it down**! You cannot keep everything in your head. (Did I say, "Write it down?") Just making sure I said this important part.) Put notes on your phone when you produce ideas. Put dates and key performance indicators in your phone calendar.

Remember the six Ps:

"Proper Planning and Preparation Prevent Piss Poor Performance"

Yes, I said "Piss" because I want you to remember it. Also, remember, philosopher, inventor, and revolutionary Benjamin Franklin said,

"If you fail to plan, you plan to fail."

American humorist Mark Twain had an affection for frogs. He captured them famously in his story of *The Celebrated Jumping Frog of Calaveras County*. Twain would advise:

"Eat a live frog first thing in the morning, and nothing worse will happen to you the rest of the day."

The **Eat That Frog** business strategy[21] uses prioritization to help people identify difficult tasks. The strategy begins with understanding that the one task you are likely to avoid is going to be the one with the biggest impact on your life.

"Simply put, some people are doing better than others because they do things differently and they do the right things right. Especially successful, happy, prosperous people use their time far, far better than the average person."[22]

Frogs offer an image for managing priorities. They are slippery and slimy. And frogs can jump from your hands and take off in different directions.

The Eat That Frog strategy serves to corner and tame those tasks. You start by finding and naming your frogs. You must know your frogs, those tasks in front of you each day. But before you allow them to jump all over, you must embrace your goals, defined as an idea a person envisions, plans, and commits to achieve.

"Executives are doers; they execute. Knowledge is useless to executives until it has been translated into deeds. But before springing into action, the executive needs to plan his course. He needs to think about desired results,

---

[21] (Tracy, 2007)
[22] (Tracy, 2007)

probable restraints, future revisions, check-in points, and implications for how he'll spend his time."[23]

So, these seven steps will help you wrangle your frogs and eat through the challenges to effective production:

1. **Set crystal clear goals**. Assign values to these expectations and name the critical characteristics.

2. **Draw pictures.** When you write your goals down, you make them real. You add dimension and avoid confusion.

3. **Put a deadline on your future.** Goals without deadlines lack urgency and encourage procrastination.

4. **Make lists.** Lists provide checkboxes that measure your progress and success.

5. **Prioritize your tasks.** You should know what frog to manage first and those other tasks you can do later. As you work out this sequence, you discover your plan to achieve.

6. **Act immediately.** Tasks do not age well. "Do first things first; do second things, not at all."[24] If you want to achieve, you must execute.

7. **Do something each day.** You must do something every day. But that action must move towards your goal. It's like doing sets of reps to build your body.

---

[23] (Drucker, 1967)
[24] (Drucker, 1967)

Okay, a sidenote: writing about eating a frog is making me lose my appetite. I ordered fried frog legs once and couldn't bring myself to eat them. They stayed on my plate. But if I had to do it today, I would do it first thing in the day to achieve my goals.

Help Who You Can

People give to churches or spiritual organizations off the top of their income. This helps others who don't have much or blesses the person who helps them.

We call this *tithing*. Both a symbolic and financial gesture, tithing thanks their Creator for blessing them with the intelligence, strength, and opportunity to make money. Giving back a part of the money they have received shows their belief that everything flows first to us from our Creator.

If you or your family are not particularly spiritual, you can still make a symbolic gesture of thanks by giving money to causes that support the things you care about. You can give to almost any cause through the thousands of charities available. Your money, no matter how little or how much, can fight homelessness, drugs, sex trafficking, etc. Or it can support music, literacy, art, and more.

Never believe that your gift is too small. Together with others around the world, it still makes a significant difference. Some charities even advertise that a $1 per day can help a person in a starving country eat for a week!

Your charity doesn't always have to offer money. You can volunteer to feed the hungry, for instance. All I am saying is that there are ways to give of yourself. You can give of your time and talent. There is always a way for all of us to help someone in need.

Summary

In this chapter, we talked about finding your passion and helping others. These are two critical pieces of the wealth picture because they hope to guide your children in their financial journeys. Too many adults end up in jobs they hate, working 40 hours or more a week doing things that don't bring them joy. We don't want that for our kids. Their work lives should be a part of their whole lives, not something that interrupts their lives. Giving is a part of that picture because people who are content in their lives look for ways to give back. Teaching your child how to be charitable will help build long-term character and a heart of kindness.

Step Ten

Get Your Education

"The beautiful thing about learning is that nobody can take it away from you."

— B.B. King, blues artist

Your Critical Investment in Education

You can spend your money on material possessions. It is always rewarding to buy something you can see and touch. But the more valuable things in life are the things you cannot hold in your hand — like education. Education is a critical investment that will pay you for years to come.

Knowledge comes from education. Self-education or formal education is essential. Take your education seriously right now, starting today! Whether your grades are fantastic or in the dumps, you can commit to being the best student you can be – now and in the future.

Education pays returns financially, culturally, intellectually, and in many other ways. You must value your education for the opportunities it presents.

Your education is free – unless you attend a tuition-based Catholic, Christian, Jewish, or private school. Once you graduate from high school, though, you will have to pay for your education. Young people work hard to get scholarships and grants to cover their college costs. Others take out loans to pay their college bills. Student loans should not be your first choice in making this a significant investment. A student loan, for example, creates debt and liability.

The more money you save, the less financial aid you will need. Talk with your parent or guardian about searching online or contacting your bank for scholarships, grants, and savings programs.

Students can apply for thousands of available scholarships and other financial aid programs. Some scholarships serve minority students and military veterans.

As you get closer to college, around age 15, start researching available sources of money, compiling a list of the ones that apply to you, and noting the deadlines. Then get to work applying. Apply for everything; much money goes unclaimed because people fail to apply.

Pay attention to smaller scholarships. Some are $50 scholarships; some are $500. You may not get the $5,000 scholarship but still receive several ten $50 scholarships. They all help and will add up.

Community College

Local community colleges save you money. Tuition is much lower than at a traditional university. I agree with those families that encourage kids to spend the first two years at a community college, completing their introductory courses before transferring to a university.

Trade School

College is only one way to become financially successful as an adult. If you don't want to go to college because you'd rather learn a trade, it doesn't make sense to take on tens of thousands of dollars in debt to go.

Trade schools graduate cosmeticians, mechanics, plumbers, electricians, nurses, medical technicians, IT specialists, and people in other technical careers every year without the expense of going to a traditional college. Careers in police, fire, and first responder jobs provide a vigorous education. These jobs are in high demand and pay significant wages. Trade schools are a great possibility.

Online Learning

Universities offer programs and degrees online, most of which are costly. But you can free college-level classes at:

- edx.org.
- Quantic.edu
- Uopeople.edu
- Coursera.com
- Online.hillsdale.edu

We are fortunate that the internet offers additional valuable learning at https://www.youtube.com/and https://www.khanacademy.org/. And it helps if you look for employers who support lifelong learning.

Due Diligence

In my humble opinion, everyone should try college for at least a year to gain what it offers. Exposure to new people who don't look or think like you and learning about diverse cultures help you widen your understanding of the world. Many people consider these ventures the best times of their lives, and the friendships they gain can last a lifetime.

Fortunately, you have information at your fingertips. You can search the internet on any subject and watch videos if that works for you.

The internet also lets you research careers. For instance, the U.S. Bureau of Labor Statistics reports on employment, job descriptions, and pay ranges throughout the country. You can access extensive data at https://www.bls.gov/ or explore career opportunities at https://www.indeed.com/.

Due Diligence prepares you to ask better-informed questions. Trust me; people know whether you have done the work that shows genuine interest, passion, and commitment.

Your education is essential, so value it. Work hard before graduating high school, trade school, or college.

Remember your financial education.

You must never neglect your financial education. Stay on top of your money, so you always know your financial picture.

Things constantly change in the financial world. I know studying and learning are demanding. But expanding and strengthening your financial literacy over time is necessary for long-term wealth building. You must stay on top of it!

You may wish there were an easier way, and you didn't have to learn so much. But these real-time issues affect you now and in the future. So, it would be best if you familiarized yourself with these economic terms:

- **GDP (Gross Domestic Product):** "Gross domestic product (GDP) is the total monetary or market value of all the finished goods and services produced within a country's borders in a specific period. As a broad measure of overall domestic production, it functions as a comprehensive scorecard of a given country's economic health."[25]

- **Recession:** "A recession is a significant decline in economic activity that lasts for months or even years. Experts declare a recession when a nation's economy experiences negative gross domestic product (GDP), rising levels of unemployment, falling retail sales, and contracting measures of income and manufacturing for an extended period. Recessions are considered an unavoidable part of the

---

[25] (Fernando, Boyle, & Rathburn, 2022)

business cycle—or the regular cadence of expansion and contraction that occurs in a nation's economy."[26]

- **Inflation:** Economic inflation occurs when prices go up. "If it feels like your dollar doesn't go quite as far as it used to, the reason is inflation, which describes the gradual rise in prices and slow decline in buying power of your money over time."[27]

- **Depression:** "An economic depression is a period of sharp and sustained decline in economic activity that typically includes negative gross domestic product growth and a substantial rise in unemployment, poverty, and homelessness. During economic depressions, the stock market drops significantly, and there is a large uptick in personal and business bankruptcies."[28]

Learning about money is fun, and I hope you find it fun, too. Once you know this, you will find it easier.

Talk about your financial education with friends and family – and follow my advice. You can have a blast learning about money.

It ALWAYS SEEMS IMPOSSIBLE UNTIL IT'S DONE.
NELSON MANDELA

However, there is no such thing as a shortcut to financial knowledge and wealth. Even if you have a crystal ball and can predict the winning lottery number, it does not promise long-term wealth. Too often, people have tried

---

[26] (Rodeck & Curry, 2022)
[27] (Schmidt & Curry, 2022)
[28] (Duggan, 2022)

get-rich-quick schemes and found that they were worse off than before they started.

Lottery winners often go broke after winning big payouts because they have not developed good money habits and the proper discipline to sustain wealth. Money only stays in the hands of someone who manages it appropriately; money runs from people who mishandle it.

You have heard horror stories of people who won the lottery and then lost it quickly, right? These people receive big winnings before they are prepared. They find money amplifies their weaknesses.

Will you do what is necessary to ensure that more money doesn't equal more problems for you? I know that the concepts you are learning are pathways to wealth. But here is a brief list of people ruined by having wealth:

- **Billy Bob Harrell Jr.:** A Pentecostal preacher working as a stock boy at Home Depot had his prayers answered when he hit a $31 million jackpot in 1997. At first, life was good, with Billy Bob buying a ranch, six other homes, and some new cars. But like many others who win the lottery, he couldn't say no when people asked for a handout. His life ended tragically.

- **Jack Whittaker:** The winner of the largest Powerball payout of its time, Jack Whittaker, already had $17 million from his business enterprises. "But in the years following his Powerball hit, his life took a seemingly cursed turn: He had hundreds of thousands of dollars stolen from him, endured multiple family tragedies — had people try to drug him, saw his home burn down, and turned into a first-class jerk."[29]

It just makes sense to refrain from broadcasting the money you have. You'd think people would be happy for you, but they get jealous. They need to realize they can build a financial portfolio just as you did.

1. Building a legacy is about being financially savvy. Book smarts and financial smarts are two separate things. You can have one without the other. But if you are not financially wise, you will live to regret it. Be a good person who is also wealthy and intelligent.

2. Those who have trouble in school, whether it's formal schooling in high school or college or learning in general, should not fear. Everything gets easier as you practice it. Pick one financial area and develop it. The one you think is the most fun or exciting and start there. You can add on later as you feel more comfortable.

3. Whatever you do, don't sell yourself short. Some of the best-known financial and business wizards were not great learners:

    -   Whoopi Goldberg has dyslexia but has conquered the stage, screen, and television.

    -   Elon Musk has Asperger's Syndrome yet leads landmark technology empires.

    -   Bill Gates dropped out of college but created Microsoft.

    -   Thomas Edison was kicked out of school at 12 and still pioneered electricity applications.

---

[29] (Kaplan, 2020)

- Albert Einstein won the Nobel Prize in Physics despite a learning disability.

I highly recommend taking at least one class from the list of free courses. Studies show that the brain requires work, challenges, and knowledge to stay fresh and sharp. But beyond that, taking classes helps you see that lifelong education has value.

Summary

The time to start saving for your kids' education is yesterday. College fees go up every year on average. So be sure to start no matter how old your child is. It might also be fun to take a course with your child on one of the free platforms. Show up with your notebook and sharpened pencils as you sit around the dining room table, looking at the course online with your child. Take it seriously. They will laugh at first, but the fact that you are taking your role as a student seriously will help your kids do the same.

How much do you know?

1. Which of the following defines *diversification*?

   A. Money your aunt gave you
   B. Different states
   C. More than one cultural
   D. More than one type of investment

2. An investor is which of the following:

   A. Someone who spends money on clothes to look fashionable
   B. Someone who saves money to spend it all summer
   C. Someone who spends money in expectation of cash in return
   D. All the above

3. What are the three types of banks:

   _____

   _____

   _____

   _____

   _____

4. Explain the difference between the "thirds" method of saving, the "fourths" method, the "ten percent" method, and the "little bit each day" savings methods.

_____

_____

_____

_____

_____

"Celebrating success is okay, but it is more important to heed the lessons of failure."

- Bill Gates, co-founder of Microsoft

Conclusion

"Pretty good report, isn't it? Do you think I can make some serious moolah with this?"

"Money and power don't change you; They just further expose your true self.

- Jay Z

One Giant Step

You've taken a big step toward building your legacy. Learn everything you can about money and how to earn and invest. People who have money love to share their knowledge. Once you have improved your financial literacy, you have no more excuses. The 18th-century American poet and philosopher Henry Wadsworth Longfellow said as much in

> ## *"Excuses are the tools of the incompetent that build monuments to nothing.*
>
> ## *Those who specialize in them seldom succeed at anything else."*

Wealth is meant to be passed down from generation to generation. Each generation should be thinking about the one coming after it.

One old saying goes, "Leave the woodpile higher than you found it." In days when firewood was the only source of heat for warmth, cooking, and washing, every home had a woodpile. Somebody had to chop down a tree and then split the wood into smaller pieces.

Families would burn the wood throughout the day and night, but they had to keep the woodpile high. So, the rule was that family members would chop wood before taking wood away from the woodpile.

Imagine how different your life would be if, when you were born, you already had money in the bank, a house, land, stocks, bonds, or other assets. It would change everything for you.

Passing wealth down from one generation to the next means passing down assets and but also knowledge. There are basic principles you must accept today. Too many adults wait until they have grown up to realize this. Your parents want you to do better. And they want you to teach these concepts to your children.

The adults in your life will confirm the following:

1. You can do anything you put your mind to.

2. All things are possible – if you work hard.

3. Knowledge is power.

4. Never sign for anyone's debt. Don't be a co-signer — not even for family and friends.

5. There is safety in "wise" counsel. Get advice about your money decisions. Never make a big money move alone.

"Every day is a bank account, and time is our currency. No one is rich, no one is poor, we've got 24 hours each!"

- Christopher Rice, 21st-century novelist

---

6. Don't ever be afraid to ask for your money from people or companies that owe you.

7. Let people help you to be successful.

8. Be bold and ask questions after doing your due diligence.

9. You must accept responsibility for your financial success or failure, no matter the circumstances.

10. Don't get into high car payment debt. You must have a family car to drive if you want to record your second vehicle as a business expense.

"A wise person should have money in their head, not in their heart."

— Jonathan Swift, 18th-century Irish satirist

11. Understand all company and employee benefits. Don't leave employee meetings covering health and retirement benefits before you understand them fully.

12. Shop for discounts and use coupons on all products and services. Coupons are money.

    Rebates and apps that help you save money could save you thousands of dollars a year.

13. Develop a saving versus spending mindset. Put your savings on autopilot. Once you start focusing on saving, it becomes a contagious habit.

14. Don't try to keep up with other people's success. Just because someone gets a new BMW doesn't mean you need to get one. If it's out of your budget, you don't have to keep up with "the Joneses."

"What we want to do is what we are meant to do. When we do what we are meant to do, money comes to us, doors open for us, we feel useful, and the work we do feels like play."

– Julia Cameron, American teacher, author, and filmmaker

15.   Live within your budget. Increase your financial standing in the future.

16. Be happy for those with more than you, and be mindful, grateful, and thankful for what you have.

17.   Pay all your monthly bills on time to keep your credit score high.

18.   Check all the bills you get — especially healthcare — to ensure they have charged you correctly.

19. Keep and review all receipts using a fancy filing system, an app, or a box into which you throw them. Just save them!

20.   Drugs will halt your life and your money. Alcohol is one of the most insidious drugs because it is socially acceptable. Yes, alcohol is a drug. My personal opinion

is to avoid it! It can cause so many problems in your life.

"You are where you are today because you stand on somebody's shoulders. And wherever you are heading, you cannot get there by yourself. If you stand on the shoulders, you have a joint responsibility to live your life so that others may stand on your shoulders. It's the quid pro quo of life. We exist temporarily through what we take, but we live forever through what we give."

- Vernon Jordon, American business executive, and Civil Rights activist attorney

---

Robert Smith, America's richest Black billionaire, paid off an entire class's student loans ($34 million) at Morehouse College and will pay off their parent's debt, too. Mr. Smith advised the students,

---

"Fight through problems. You need to solve easy issues now to solve complex problems later."

Don't burn bridges. In other words, don't destroy anyone's path, connections, reputation, opportunities, and so on, particularly intentionally. Even if you are fired in the worst way, take care not to burn your bridges with smart comments on the way out. You never know whom you will meet again or need in the future.

You must crawl before you walk!

Once you take the time to learn about money, problems become manageable, like walking after crawling.

Always remember that money is a tool to better your life and not a tool to impress people. Money will follow you throughout your life in one form or another.

As we have discussed, you cannot define true wealth in dollars and cents. Money-free societies continue to prove that every day. Even if you had decided to live out in the bush in a moneyless culture, you would have to deal with money or the exchange of goods.

- The Yanomami Indians of the Amazon in northern Brazil have survived upheavals for centuries, including when slavers hunted them and vested interests wanted to "integrate" them. They grow their food, fish for what their families need, and barter any added harvest among themselves. They are a society of an estimated 35,000 today and live in small communities in their respective villages numbering 30 to 400 individuals – without cash.[30]

- The people of the Milne Bay Province of Papua New Guinea exchange personal jewelry made of shells and natural materials. "While exchanging the goods, they listen to each other's stories and dilemmas and offer help or advice when needed. The underlying value system and cultural custom in the KULA Ring are a 'display of greatness' Giving is valued as highly honorable and as more noble than solely receiving."[31]

Such tribes show that *family* is their most significant wealth. It might be nice to live in a society where money is unimportant. But if you remain in this highly commercialized society, you must understand money and learn how to deal with it.

---

[30] (John, 2018)
[31] (Kula Ring)

Money is the perfect amplifier.

I have spent space here discussing the issues that may confuse you regarding money — morals, values, and ethics. I know these principles work, so I am careful to encourage you to take care of the rest of your life before the money starts rolling in big time.

We have talked about how money enhances who we already are. As we conclude, it would be wise to revisit that concept in more detail. Money is the perfect amplifier. You know what an amplifier is, right? It's that thing you connect to the microphone or stereo to make sounds louder. It doesn't change sound; it only makes it louder, bigger, and more pronounced.

That is all money will do for you. It won't change who you are. It will only extend the reach of your attitude, mindset, and philosophy. It will make your voice bigger, louder, and more pronounced. That's why it is vital to hone your character before you get the money.

Money won't make you a better person. It won't make you worse. It will just exaggerate the traits you currently have. People who are investors, savers, and givers will do so at a much higher level once they have more money. People who are rude, stingy, and mean will only demonstrate more of that.

You have heard horror stories of people who won the lottery and then lost it all, right?

This book will improve your financial literacy. Research has found that "financial literacy is low; fewer than one-third of young adults possess basic knowledge of interest rates, inflation, and risk diversification."[32] Book smarts and financial smarts are two separate things. You can have one without the other. But if you are not financially astute, you will live to regret it.

Be an intelligent, wealthy person who is also good!

Be kind to people. Treat the person who cleans the restrooms with the same respect as you treat others. Once you have the money, you don't want to be rude, arrogant, or impossible to deal with.

Keep the people close who were there at the beginning of your success and who love you. Wealthy people always have opportunists trying to get at them, so beware. Opportunists want what you can do for them. They want to be associated with you for the image.

However, the people surrounding you shape your character and reputation, so choose your friends well. Be a good citizen, and if you choose between right and wrong, always do what's right.

My grandmother said, "There is no accounting for *class*," meaning you can't put a price on a quality person or thing that displays impressive and excellence.

---

[32] (Lusardi, Mitchell, & Curto, 2010)

Madame C.J. Walker, an African American entrepreneur, business leader, philanthropist, and activist, told her audiences:

> ## *"Don't sit down and wait for opportunities to come. Get up and make them."*

In the end, the only wealth and legacy you have in this life are your health, the love of your family, and the good you do in the world. The great jazz singer Billie Holiday once sang,

---

> ## *"God bless the child that's got his own."*

Money is just the bonus, like a cherry on an ice cream sundae. So be healthy − mentally, physically, emotionally, and spiritually − in the content of your character. Mahatma Gandhi, the immortal Indian philosopher, and revolutionary, used a Chinese proverb:

> ## *"Your beliefs become your thoughts,*

Your thoughts become your words,

Your words become your actions,

Your actions become your habits,

Your habits become your values,

Your values become your destiny. "

"Everybody can be great...because anybody can serve. You don't have to have a college degree to serve. You don't have to make your subject and verb agree to serve. You only need a heart full of grace. A soul generated by love." — Dr. Martin Luther King Jr., "The Drum Major Instinct" Sermon.

No matter what, don't let money corrupt your heart and soul. When bad things happen financially, people who don't have integrity will do whatever it takes to recover. They will take advantage of their customers, lie to their distributors, and cheat whomever they need to recover from their financial loss. But you won't do that because you have integrity! Stay true to your values!

You should use the money to help yourself, your family, and others. If you do that, you will have a legacy you can be proud of.

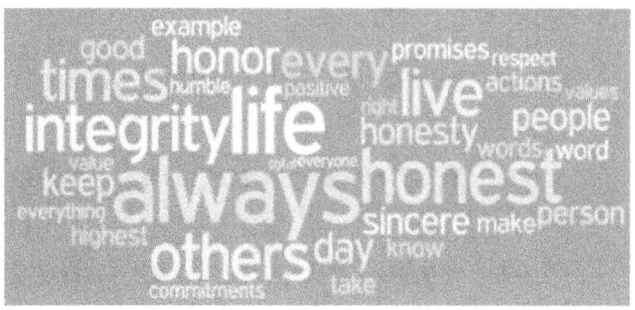

Here's a poem to memorize and live your life by:

IF

by Rudyard Kipling

IF you can keep your head when all about you

Are losing theirs and blaming it on you,

IF you can trust yourself when all men doubt you,

But make allowance for their doubting too,

IF you can wait and not be tired by waiting,

Or being lied about, don't deal in lies,

Or being hated, don't give way to hating,

And yet don't look too good, nor talk too wise:

IF you can dream — and not make dreams your master,

IF you can think — and not make thoughts your aim,

IF you can meet with Triumph and Disaster

And treat those two impostors just the same,

IF you can bear to hear the truth you've spoken

Twisted by knaves to make a trap for fools,

Or watch the things you gave your life to, broken,

And stoop and build them up with worn-out tools:

IF you can make one heap of all your winnings

And risk it on one turn of pitch-and-toss,

And lose, and start again at your beginnings

And never breathe a word about your loss,

IF you can force your heart and nerve and sinew

To serve your turn long after they are gone,

And so, hold on when there is nothing in you

Except the Will which says to them: 'Hold on!'

IF you can talk with crowds and keep your virtue

Or walk with Kings — nor lose the common touch,

IF neither foes nor loving friends can hurt you,

IF all men count with you, but none too much,

IF you can fill the unforgiving minute

With sixty seconds' worth of distance run,

Yours is the Earth and everything that's in it,

And—which is more—you'll be a Man, my son! *

* You can substitute "woman" for "man" and "daughter" for "son."

Tip

The book may be almost over, but education never stops. Hopefully, they will pass these concepts and lessons down to their children. Everything you need may not be in this one book. You must continue to learn more about finances, trusts, tax write-offs etc.

Get involved. Help your kids think of business and investment opportunities. Pick stocks together. Go treasure hunting for rare coins at estate sales. Have fun with this!

Everything you need may not be in this one book. You must continue to learn more about finances, trusts, tax write-offs etc.

Blueprint to start and maintain a real business

What will you do if your business takes off? You must get serious about making it legal and putting the pieces in place to run it.

At first, it may seem complicated to get going so, I have broken it down into 10 goals to target.

GOAL ONE
Give the business a name

Of course, you will name your business. It should be obvious why you should give the company a solid and marketable name. Choose a name you are proud of, one that makes you feel it communicates who you are and what you do.

Unfortunately, so many people don't. They choose names that are hard to pronounce, confusing, or silly. Of course, a silly name works if it helps people remember you. But you want people to be laughing *with* you rather than *at* you.

If you plan to grow and expand, you must have a name that can grow with you over the years. Consumers must be able to identify your product or service quickly. You will use your name for advertising on a website or social media. Your name becomes a growth tool.

Do not rush this decision. The correct best name for your business will come to you over time.

- It should be short unless there is a strategy in making it long.

- It should be easy to spell and remember. If they can't spell the name, people will move on to the competitor who chose a more straightforward expression.

- It would help if you captured the product or service in the name, like Scotch® Tape or Band-Aid®. This can increase awareness.

- You may even create an innovative word if it is related to your product or service. Examples include Netflix, Groupon®, and Pinterest.

It helps if you can remove your ego from the naming process. Just because you love your family name doesn't mean you should attach it to your business. You can use the family name only if you already have a large following that will instantly recognize your name.

Think of it as a book title. The book's title is the first thing people see and what they must say if they recommend it to others. If it doesn't interest the potential reader, they won't flip the book over to read the description. Some businesses get it right, while others get it very wrong.

BEST NAMES FOR A BUSINESS

- Fiverr – Hire freelancers for as little as five dollars!

- Google – It's just fun to say!

- Coca-Cola – alliteration always works!

- Ikea – rolls off the tongue!

- Verizon – combines *veritas* and *horizon*!

- Skype – short, sweet, simple!

- Amazon – mighty sounding name!

WORST NAMES FOR A BUSINESS

- Bunghole Liquors

- Passmore Gas

- Dumas Tacos

- Poopsie's Pizza

- Stubb's Prosthetics and Orthotics

- Sam & Ella's Chicken Palace

- Amigone's Funeral Home

You might opt for a **Business Name Generator** such as www.businessnamegenerator.com or www.wix.com. Form a Focus Group – friends, family, and strangers, too – for feedback on select business names. Offer the group a list of four or five titles, including your favorites. Then listen to their input. Don't be stubborn and choose a name you like just because you want it. Make sure your customers will like it and will understand what you are selling.

Once you decide on a name, you must check to see if it is available. If you plan to incorporate, check with the Secretary of State in the state where you plan to establish your business.

Check for trademarks if you plan to sell your product or service nationally or globally. You don't want to create a successful business only to discover that you have infringed on someone else's right to that name. At the very least, check to see if the name is available for you to file a trademark.

It takes money to apply for a trademark, but as soon as you make a profit, file for a brand name so no one else can take it. Believe me, you want to be sure you own the full rights to your name.

If you plan to be a sole proprietor and want to use a name that is not yours, check with your county office to see if the DBA or assumed name is available.

DBA = Doing Business As

You must have a website if you plan to stay in business for a long time. A **Domain Name** is your website address. It is essential to check to see if the address is available. Or you can bid to buy an existing domain name.

GOAL TWO

Find a business address

Every business needs a headquarters or location where it can be reached. The best type of business address is a physical location. If you have a brick-and-mortar store or facility where everything takes place, this will serve as your business address in most cases. If you have a factory where you produce your product, the factory address might be your business address.

Alternatively, you can choose an office located in a low-rent area. Of course, challenges may come with these areas. They may have poor visibility, accessibility, and convenience. It may be in a high-crime area. But if your business does not require customers to visit in person, opting for a low-rent location may be a promising idea when starting.

For example, if your business is an ice cream store, you should not set the business in a remote or dangerous place. People will not come. The rents may be lower, but you must always protect your employees, equipment, and supplies.

We find an increasing number of businesses conducted online. But even they require an address for legal reasons. They might choose a P.O. Mailbox, UPS box, or a "virtual office."

Renting space in a shared workspace office has potential. These virtual offices can help present your company as a legitimate business. They offer office services, something as simple as receiving mail. These physical locations may also provide you with office space, furniture, telephones, and conference rooms. Shared receptionists perfect your business credibility.

The upside to using your home address is that there will be little or no added cost for rent, and you can write off part of your housing cost as a business expense. But the advantages end here. You may find it difficult to mentally separate your business time from your personal time if your business is in your home. You may find it harder to focus and concentrate. These personal challenges present only the beginning.

You do not want your customers to have 24-hour access. You will find that work constantly bleeds into home life. You may want to vacation or walk around the block. And you want to enjoy your weekends.

GOAL THREE

Choose an entity

This section is for educational purposes only. Laws may vary from state to state. You should consult a CPA or an attorney if you have any questions about the information provided in this step.

I recommend forming a Personal Board of Directors. Form an advisory board of friends and family with management skills and experience. All business owners need advice on Human Resources, accounting, strategic plans, and more.

When you start a business, you should start selling more than just a product or service. You must commit to launching your company. Like a baby, it needs to be born. You must register it with the state, give it a name, and have an actual birthdate.

You begin by selecting how you want your business organized and reported. Your organization may change as your business grows over time.

The following list covers the common business frameworks:

- **Sole Proprietorship**: Most businesses start as Sole Proprietorships. Sole Proprietorships include mom-and-pop grocery stores and restaurants, gig workers, and freelancers. Small retail and online businesses remain Sole Proprietorships as long as they exist.

  As a **Sole Proprietor,** you own the business and have the sole right to its profits. But it also means you have sole responsibility for its debts and liabilities.

  Sole Proprietors should register an EIN (Employer Identification Number) and DBA (Doing Business As) for accounting, taxation, and other standard business practices.

- **Limited Liability Corporation (LLC)**: The **LLC** designation makes the business − not the owner − responsible for its own debts and liabilities. If, for example, someone sues the LLC, the owner protects his or her personal assets. The business's assets remain at risk, but the LLC status protects the owner's personal property.

Think of it this way: imagine you are eleven years old. While outside playing baseball with friends, you break someone's car windshield. The car owner might hold your parents responsible for replacing the broken windshield. That's a sole proprietorship.

Now imagine that this accident occurs on your 18th birthday. You are technically an adult. If you break that windshield, the car owner cannot hold your parents accountable – even if you still live at home and don't have a job. That's how an LLC works.

Getting an EIN (Employer Identification Number) and a DBA (Doing Business As) helps retain your privacy. I will share more about these later in the section.

- A **Partnership** brings two or more persons into the business structure and ownership. The partners share both the profit and the liabilities, including the lawsuits. Partnership agreements have complex pieces. You want to clarify what everyone must do in the partnership, framing those responsibilities in writing. You need an experienced lawyer to draw up the partnership agreement.

- A **Corporation** requires more advice, paperwork, and expense. The law treats a corporation as a legal "person." A corporate status further distances you from company debts and liabilities.

However, it also minimizes your personal connection with the passion that launched the business in the first place.

As with any business structure, you want to avoid commingling business funds with personal expenses. You must refrain from paying private bills with company money. It is okay to pay yourself but keep good records. This is necessary to protect your personal assets and avoid liability for business debt and lawsuits. Laws and benefits may vary from state to state, so you should consult a CPA for further tax implications or an attorney if you have any questions about liability.

A business owner should understand each business entity structure's advantages to determine which best serves their business goals.

GOAL FOUR

Get an EIN

The **IRS (Internal Revenue Service)** assigns your business an **EIN – an Employee Identification Number**, a nine-digit number that functions like your personal Social Security number.

You will need an EIN to open a bank account, get a business license, build business credit, pay taxes, do business with the government, and secure a **DUN (Data Universal Number)** number.

Despite its name, you do not need to have employees get an EIN. It is for self-employed freelancers, corporations, LLCs, Partnerships, nonprofits, and Sole Proprietors. You need an EIN on the day you start to take your business seriously

There are four ways to get the EIN:

- File online at https://www.irs.gov/.

- Call 267-941-1099 if you are an international client.

- Fax the SS4 application form to 855-641-6935.

- Locate, print, and complete the SS4 form and mail it to E. I. N. Operations, Cincinnati, Ohio 45999.

You should receive your EIN number by mail in about four weeks, by fax in about four days, and online instantly. However you file, you should save the confirmation letter as proof. If you have any questions, contact the IRS directly.

GOAL FIVE

Be contactable

Make sure your voicemail sounds highly professional. If you use a cell phone and are not in a convenient place to talk, move to a place without background noise before returning the call.

List your local number in local and relevant directories so lenders, creditors, insurance companies, vendors, and customers can find you.

GOAL SIX

Get a business bank account

A **Business Bank Account** separates your personal and business transactions. This helps you monitor revenue and expenses and can help supply a level of personal asset protection. You should never (I repeat, never!) comingle business and private funds.

It's time to open a Business Account when you plan to launch a business, increase revenue, or keep your financial records in order. You can research and compare potential banks by visiting the branch or their website. Pay attention to the customer service they offer because that is what you will have to deal with if you have an issue that requires their help. Ask about fees. And investigate ways they may increase revenue flow options. You want customers to have choices when making payments.

To open a business account, you will need your personal identification, proof of your EIN, and your corporation or LLC registration. Be sure to deposit as much as possible and as often as possible to increase your bank rating. Stay with the same bank to develop a relationship and improves your lending opportunities.

GOAL SEVEN

Get a business license

Most locations in the U. S. require a Business License. States, counties, and cities issue business licenses. Most business licenses are issued in the city where the business lists its address.

Licensing requirements may be as simple as supplying information and paying a fee. Other licenses require special training and a background check.

- Refrain from assuming what you must or should do to get a business license.

- Refrain from assuming that licensing requirements are too easy or too difficult.

- You will know once you check. You can visit a website or make a phone call. Business licenses come in different forms:

- Businesses that sell their product on the street at multiple locations within the city limits require a **Peddler's License**.

- A **General Business License** applies to most brick-and-mortar locations. Hair stylists, food servers, plumbers, electricians, and other services may require documented training and licensing. And cities break these licenses down based on the variety of goods or services offered.

- Cities will zone certain types of business into defined geographic areas. They may designate Commercial zones for retail or offices, Industrial zones for manufacturing, Agricultural zones for farming, and Residential zones for houses, apartments, and condominiums.

- Cities may require a business license for **home-based businesses.**

A government can refuse to issue a business license to enterprises inviting high consumer traffic, extensive parking, or large storage space for inventory and supplies. It can also refuse to license or segregate locations for alcohol-based businesses and adult entertainment. States that collect sales tax may also require businesses to register with that state.

Business License

Check with your state government for most professional licenses. Examples include licenses for real estate or insurance sales. Remember that requirements and fees may vary from state to state, and most licenses require a certain amount of educational training. You must consult your city, county, and state governments for detailed information.

GOAL EIGHT

Secure a DUNS number

Dun & Bradstreet is the oldest and largest of the three major business credit reporting agencies. Dun & Bradstreet issues the unique nine-digit **DUNS number (Data Universal Numbering System)** identifying  your business. Vendors and suppliers can check on your business credit with the DUNS number. The Federal Government uses it to track how the business distributes federal funds, secures government contracts, or applies for most government funding, including grants.

Every business starts with a zero score. The highest score is one hundred, and vendors consider any number above 80 a good score. Timely payments to your creditors affect the score favorably.

You can get a free DUNS number within 30 days. You can pay to receive one within 5 days. If you tell them you plan to do business with the government, you can get a free DUNS number within 3 days. And you can apply for your DUNS number at https://www.dnb.com/.

D&B may try to up-sell their services, but you can buy a number without buying more. Once you have a number, you must have your personal and company information available to set up security questions. You can log in a specific number of times each month to check what your suppliers report about your credit.

Goal NINE

Maximize your reach

In this digital age, a business must appear across multiple social media accounts, including Facebook, Instagram, Pinterest, Twitter, Yelp, and more. These digital platforms allow customers to voice their opinions of your product and service.

A successful business depends on a robust website, an online presence with vivid visuals, and persuasive language. An effective website helps people navigate through product detail, customer endorsements, and online purchase convenience.

Having an "internet presence" means "being found online." This starts with creating a robust website. As your business grows, you may recruit a Website Manager to design, manage, and sustain your site.

A dynamic website gives you complete control over the information shared on the internet. It builds your brand, sells a product or service, attracts customers, and brings your business one step closer to being recession-proof.

As a new business, you can create an effective website with Google, Wix, and GoDaddy – *for free!* You can build a basic e-commerce website and host it for less than $1 a day with little experience. And you can be up and running with your website in less than an hour.

You start by registering a **Domain Name**. A Domain Name creates a personalized website address connected to your website's "physical address." Domain names consist of a name and an extension, "the combination of letters, numbers, and symbols someone types in their browser to access a specific web address directly."[33]

Familiar domain names include .com, .gov, .net, and .org. You can find and register your domain name at www.domains.google.com. This platform lets you enter a business name. It lists the options in use and those available for purchase. This analysis may require you to rethink your business name or buy an already registered domain name.

You also must build a business profile on Google Chrome, Microsoft Edge, and GoDaddy platforms to enhance customer access to your business, products, services, and sales.

You want to increase your **SEO (Search Engine Optimization)**. SEO requires proficiency in how websites and browsers work. The

---

[33] (Miller, 2021)

website's language must meet search optimization standards. For instance, internet browsers prefer single-syllable words, simple sentences, and short paragraphs. You may need to outsource website language and blogs to maximize your online presence.

GOAL TEN

Secure business credit

There are two ways to start using business credit: *with* a personal guarantee or *without* a personal guarantee. Regardless of which way you start, the long-term goal should be to have as little debt attached to the business as possible with a personal guarantee.

- Starting a business *with* a personal guarantee is not difficult − if you have good credit. But as the cosigner for your business, you are liable for the business's debt. So, a default on the business credit can affect your personal credit.

    Moreover, if you do not set the business up correctly, any credit you get would just be personal credit; you would not build business credit.

- To start business credit *without* a personal guarantee, follow the setup steps provided in this section. Remember, when choosing a name, avoid using DBAs because multiple DBAs with the same name can cause confusion and denials. When choosing a business address, do not use a PO Box, UPS mailbox, or a personal mailbox.

"If you have a good personal credit score, qualifying for a business credit card may be easy, even as a startup."[34] You should "open a business credit card with a company that reports account activity to the business credit bureaus."[35]

If you follow these steps, you will have a business credit profile. This may be enough to secure instant credit with vendors without a personal guarantee. The owner's personal credit will not matter.

Having business credit means different things to different businesses. If you just want to finance inventory, you can contact each vendor directly, asking what you must do to earn their credit. Vendors often will give your business credit instantly with only an EIN and a 411 listing. Some suppliers may require you to prepay your first order. And others may just ask you to order one of their catalogs.

Vendors and suppliers usually start the business off with a net account. This allows your business to receive goods under the expectation that you will pay within 30, 60, or 90 days.

Be careful with business credit. It is a tool to help start, maintain, or grow a business. Access to capital helps in building inventory,

---

[34] (Pokora & Tarvar, 2020)
[35] (Pokora & Tarvar, 2020)

securing supplies, and managing tricky situations. Do not overuse it or abuse it!

This is it. You should be well on your way by this point. Now get ready to start your LEGACY!!!

I'm sending my best wishes to each person that has read this book, and I'm rooting for you.

Thank you! P.Smith.

My Legacy ~ My Grandparents

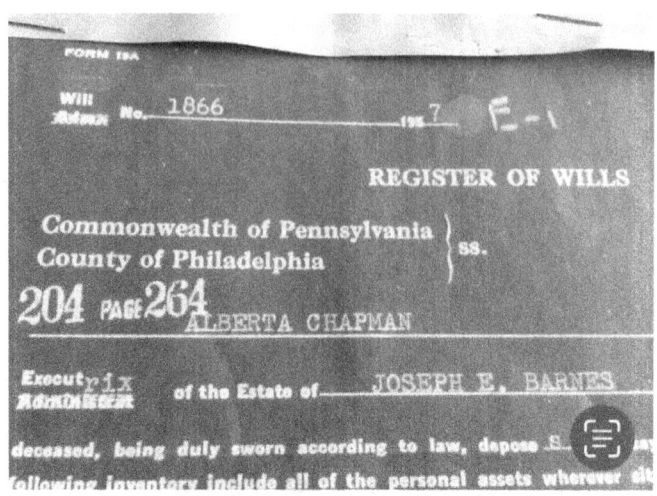

FORM 19A

Will No. 1866 19 7 E-1

REGISTER OF WILLS

Commonwealth of Pennsylvania } ss.
County of Philadelphia

204 PAGE 264 ALBERTA CHAPMAN

Executrix of the Estate of JOSEPH E. BARNES

deceased, being duly sworn according to law, depose

following inventory include all of the personal assets wherever sit

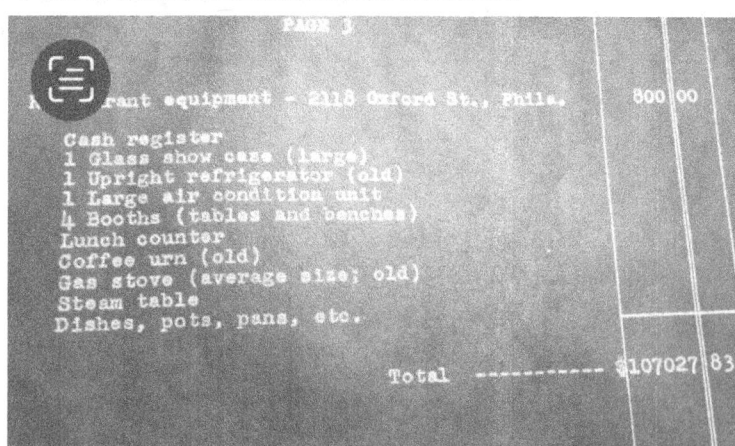

PAGE 3

rant equipment - 2118 Oxford St., Phila.   800 00

Cash register
1 Glass show case (large)
1 Upright refrigerator (old)
1 Large air condition unit
4 Booths (tables and benches)
Lunch counter
Coffee urn (old)
Gas stove (average size; old)
Steam table
Dishes, pots, pans, etc.

Total ------------ $107027 83

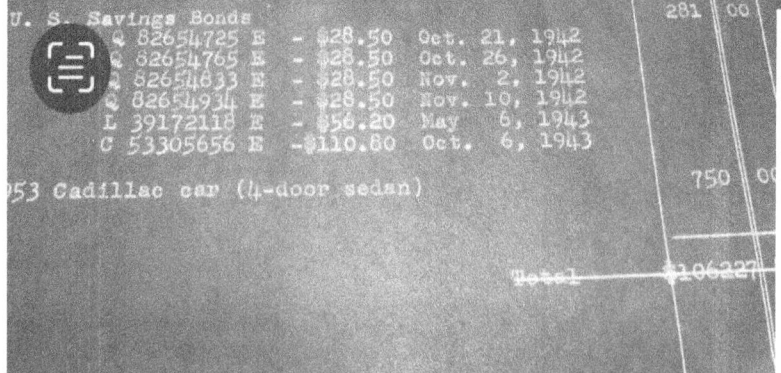

U. S. Savings Bonds   281 00
  82654725 E - $28.50 Oct. 21, 1942
  82654765 E - $28.50 Oct. 26, 1942
  82654833 E - $28.50 Nov. 2, 1942
  82654934 E - $28.50 Nov. 10, 1942
  L 39172118 E - $56.20 May 6, 1943
  C 53305656 E - $110.80 Oct. 6, 1943

53 Cadillac car (4-door sedan)   750 00

Total $106227

186

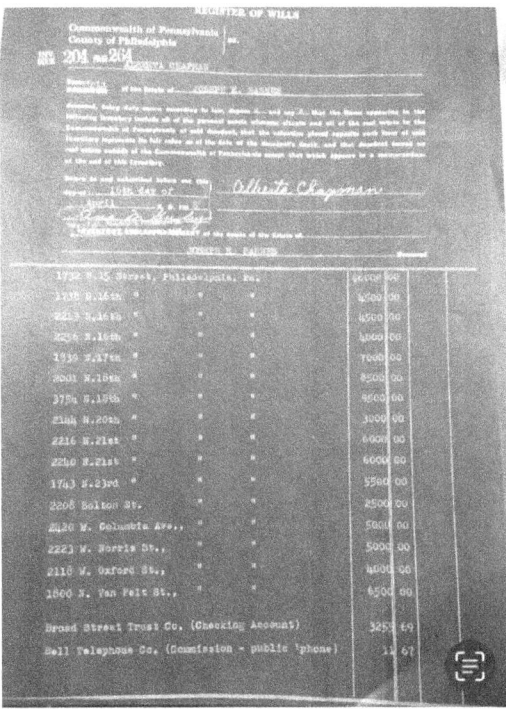

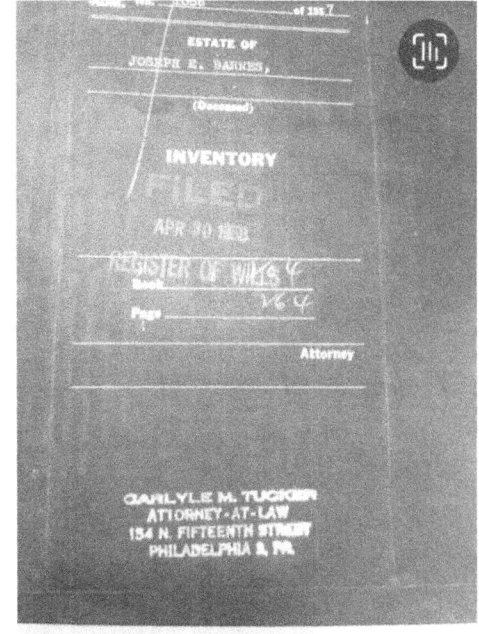

ABOUT THE AUTHOR

Born and raised in Philadelphia, Pennsylvania, Pamela Smith graduated from Penn State with a degree in Chemical Engineering Technology. Pamela worked for IBM and remains a member of Delta Sigma Theta Sorority, Inc. Author, entrepreneur, and Deaconess Pamela Smith is a mother and advocate for any who need her. She Is blessed to be called "Mom Pam." by many.

She is the granddaughter of a prominent 1960s Philadelphia restaurant owner, Joseph Barnes, a success at a time when few people that looked like him prospered. His business dealings produced over a half million dollars in assets in the 1960s, including 17 houses in the now-gentrified neighborhoods of North Philadelphia. Only one place is still in the family today. This inspired Pamela to write this book: to change generational mindsets. Pamela also wanted to honor her grandfather's memory.

Pamela's children and family have shared the knowledge they gained in their college studies, experience, and entrepreneurship. As a family, they wish to educate others to navigate the financial world.

Works Cited

Bobbit, F. W. (1973). The Boss [Recorded by J. Brown]. On *Black Caesar*. Universal Records, a Division of UMG Recordings, Inc.

Bradbury, R. (2022, July 5). This is how much money you need to be considered 'wealthy' in America's biggest cities. *Business Insider*. Retrieved from https://www.businessinsider.com/how-much-money-do-you-need-wealthy-us-it-depends-2022-7

Buffet, W. (n.d.). My Philanthropic Pledge. Retrieved from http://pds18.egloos.com/pds/201008/05/46/My_Philanthropic_Pledge.pdf

Carbone, N. (2012, November 27). *The Tragic Stories of the Lottery's Unluckiest Winners*. Retrieved from Time: https://newsfeed.time.com/2012/11/28/500-million-powerball-jackpot-the-tragic-stories-of-the-lotterys-unluckiest-winners/slide/janite-lee/

Conlon, E. (2022, March 2). *How to Make a Dream Board*. Retrieved from WikiHow: https://www.wikihow.com/Make-a-Dream-Board

Drucker, P. (1967). *The Effective Executive*. New York: Harper-Collins Publishers.

Duggan, W. (2022, August 7). *What Is an Economic Depression?* Retrieved from US News & World Report: https://money.usnews.com/investing/term/economic-depression

Engle, P. (2016, January 6). *21 lottery winners who blew it all*. Retrieved from Business Insider: https://www.businessinsider.com/lottery-winners-who-lost-everything-2016-1

Fernando, J., Boyle, M., & Rathbun, P. (2022, September 29). *Gross Domestic Product (GDP): Formula and How to Use It*. Retrieved from Investopedia: https://www.investopedia.com/terms/g/gdp.asp

Gallo, C. (2014, May 31). *The Maya Angelou Quote That Will Radically Improve Your Business*. Retrieved from Forbes: https://www.forbes.com/sites/carminegallo/2014/05/31/the-maya-angelou-quote-that-will-radically-improve-your-business/?sh=3fdb15d9118b

Guilford, G. (2022, July 20). *The dangerous economics of racial resentment during World War II*. Retrieved from Quartz: https://qz.com/1201502/japanese-internment-camps-during-world-war-ii-are-a-lesson-in-the-scary-economics-of-racial-resentment/

Herschfield, H., Shu, S., & Benartzi, S. (2019). Temporal Reframing and Participation in a Savings Program: A Field Experiment. *Marketing Science, 39*.

John, M. (2018, June 28). Who Are The Yanomami? *World Atlas*. Retrieved from https://www.worldatlas.com/articles/who-are-the-yanomami.html

Kahneman, D. (1999). *Well-Being: Foundations of Hedonic Psychology*. United States: Russell Sage Foundation.

Kaplan, M. (2020, July 4). *Inside expensive downward spiral of the $315 million Powerball winner*. Retrieved from New York Post: https://nypost.com/2020/07/04/downward-spiral-of-315-million-powerball-winner-jack-whittaker/

Kleinhandler, D. (2018, Oct. 19). *Generational Wealth: Why do 70% of Families Lose Their Wealth in the 2nd Generation?* Retrieved from Nasdaq: https://www.nasdaq.com/articles/generational-wealth%3A-why-do-70-of-families-lose-their-wealth-in-the-2nd-generation-2018-10

Kula Ring. (n.d.). Retrieved from Kula Society: https://kulasociety.com/kula-ring/

Lewis-Fernandez, E. (2020, December 30). *7 Must-Ask Questions in Any Negotiation*. Retrieved from Zenbusiness: https://www.zenbusiness.com/blog/negotiation-questions/

Lusardi, A., Mitchell, O., & Curto, V. (2010, June 1). Financial Literacy among the Young. *The Journal of Consumer Affairs*. doi:https://doi.org/10.1111/j.1745-6606.2010.01173.x

Mariotti, M., & Glackin, C. (2014). *Entrepreneurship and Small Business Management* (4th ed.). Pearson.

Miller, D. (2021, April 26). *What is a domain name? Everything you need to know about domain names*. Retrieved from GoDaddy: https://www.godaddy.com/garage/what-is-a-domain-name/

Moran, R. (2021, June 25). *Family Wealth: Beat The 3rd Generation Curse And Achieve Financial Longevity*. Retrieved from Tatler: https://www.tatlerasia.com/power-purpose/wealth/my-rise-and-fall-of-family-wealth-how-to-achieve-financial-longevity

Native American Ownership and Governance of Natural Resources. (2022). Retrieved from Natural Resources Revenue Data: https://revenuedata.doi.gov/how-revenue-works/native-american-ownership-governance/#:~:text=To%20understand%20current%20ownership%20of

%20Native%20American%20lands%2C,Americans%20in%20an%20effort%20to%20break%20up%20reservations.

Pena, D. (2019, July 14). Billionaire Dan Pena's Ultimate Advice for Students & Young People - HOW TO SUCCEED IN LIFE. *Motivation2Study*. Retrieved from https://www.youtube.com/watch?v=N6zqatiur3A

Pokora, B., & Tarvar, J. (2020, Dec. 21). *How To Build Business Credit In 6 Simple Steps.* Retrieved from Forbes: https://www.forbes.com/advisor/business-loans/how-to-build-business-credit/

Rodeck, D., & Curry, B. (2022, July 12). *What Is A Recession?* Retrieved from Forbes: https://www.forbes.com/advisor/investing/what-is-a-recession/

Schmidt, J., & Curry, B. (2022, August 5). *How Inflation Erodes The Value Of Your Money.* Retrieved from Forbes: https://www.forbes.com/advisor/investing/what-is-inflation/

Srinivas, V., & Goradia, U. (2015, November 10). *The future of wealth in the United States: Mapping trends in generational wealth.* Retrieved from Deloitte Insights: https://www2.deloitte.com/us/en/insights/industry/investment-management/us-generational-wealth-trends.html

Stanley, T., & Danko, W. (1996). *The Millionaire Next Door: The Surprising Secrets of America's Wealthy.* New York: Gallery Books.

Sullivan, P. (2006, January 20). *William 'Bud' Post III.* Retrieved from Washington Post: https://www.washingtonpost.com/archive/local/2006/01/20/william-bud-post-iii/e2c64b90-550d-470f-8337-d853795888bd/

Tracy, B. (2007). *Eat That Frog!: 21 Great Ways to Stop Procrastinating and Get More Done in Less Time.* San Francisco: Berrett-Koehler Publishers, Inc.

Vega, N. (2022, May 10). *In 1999, Warren Buffett was asked what you should do to get as rich as him—his advice still applies toda.* Retrieved from CNBC Make It: https://www.cnbc.com/2021/07/23/warren-buffetts-advice-from-1999-on-how-he-would-invest-10000-dollars.html

www.ingramcontent.com/pod-product-compliance
Lightning Source LLC
Chambersburg PA
CBHW070330220526
45467CB00001B/110